MW00456168

"If you're going to scale up, you should also know how to step out. If the exit price is under $25 million, this book has all the right tools."

—Verne Harnish, founder, Entrepreneurs' Organization (EO); bestselling author of *Scaling Up: How a Few Companies Make It... and Why the Rest Don't* (Rockefeller Habits 2.0)

"Every business sale is a series of complex negotiations and emotions. Jessica Fialkovich breaks it down into fundamental steps to help you maximize value and prepare for your inevitable exit. Any seller with this book will have a real advantage."

—Bob House, president, BizBuySell

"There's a reason why Jessica and her team have been Transworld Business Advisors' #1 for so long, and their customer satisfaction ratings are through the roof. They know what it takes to sell a business and get you top dollar. All the secrets are in this book."

—Andrew Cagnetta, CEO, Transworld Business Advisors; host, The Deal Board podcast; author of *Closing the Deal*

"There's a huge difference between playing a game as an amateur and playing in the NFL. This book explains how to sell your business like a pro. Jessica is the teammate you need as you exit your company, helping you keep your eye on the trophy."

—Reggie Rivers, president, Corporate Kickoff; Former NFL player

"The end goal for every business owner is to build something you could sell, whether you want to today or in the future. As Jessica points out, a successful business sale is never possible until the entrepreneur gets out of the daily grind—along with every other step she describes in this indispensable book."

—Chris Ronzio, founder and CEO, Trainual; author of *The Business Playbook: How to Document and Delegate What You Do So Your Company Can Grow Beyond You*

"You cannot successfully sell a company without knowledge and discipline. Many business owners are confused, naive, and unrealistic about selling their business, and don't appreciate the complexity of the process. This book will help you avoid incredibly costly and painful mistakes. Jessica makes it awesomely simple! For anyone even contemplating selling their company, this book is literally a must-read."

—John Spence, global business and leadership development expert; award-winning CEO; author of *Awesomely Simple: Essential Business Strategies for Turning Ideas Into Action*

"A franchise is great at teaching entrepreneurs how to build and grow your own business. But when it's time to sell, Jessica is the one who will take you to the finish line. You need this book."

—Ray Titus, CEO, United Franchise Group

"Like anything else, peak performance for selling a business requires process and discipline. All you should know can be found in these pages."

—Brent Gleason, founder and CEO, TakingPoint Leadership; bestselling author of *Embrace the Suck: The Navy SEAL Way to an Extraordinary Life*; former Navy SEAL

GETTING THE MOST FOR SELLING YOUR BUSINESS

How to Get Top Dollar for the Company You've Nurtured for Years

Jessica Fialkovich

with Anne Mary Ciminelli

FOREWORD BY KEVIN DAUM

Skyhorse Publishing

Skyhorse Publishing books may be purchased in bulk at special discounts for sales promotion, corporate gifts, fund-raising, or educational purposes. Special editions can also be created to specifications. For details, contact the Special Sales Department, Skyhorse Publishing, 307 West 36th Street, 11th Floor, New York, NY 10018 or info@skyhorsepublishing.com.

Skyhorse® and Skyhorse Publishing® are registered trademarks of Skyhorse Publishing, Inc.®, a Delaware corporation.

Visit our website at www.skyhorsepublishing.com.

10 9 8 7 6 5 4 3 2 1

Library of Congress Cataloging-in-Publication Data is available on file.

Cover design by David Ter-Avanesyan

Print ISBN: 978-1-5107-6963-2
Ebook ISBN: 978-1-5107-6964-9

Printed in the United States of America

For the entrepreneurs who work tirelessly every day to create better futures for themselves and their families.

Contents

Acknowledgments

In this book I explain that it takes a village to raise, nurture, and sell a business. Writing a book is no different. I am grateful to have such a supportive group around me that helped birth this book.

Thank you to my entire Transworld Business Advisor teams from Colorado, Dallas/Fort Worth, and Las Vegas, but especially for the help and contributions of Dustin Audet, Patrick Bombardiere, Taylor Bombardiere, Tyler Bowman, Linda Broom, Chris Cantwell, Alex Dvorak, Ali Elman, Axel Fleischi, Gary Goldwasser, Lee Grubb, Nathan Willis, and John Woodhull.

For mentorship, knowledge, and guidance: Andrew Cagnetta, Ray Titus, and Heidi Ganahl.

For getting me into the business brokerage industry and continuing to support my every move: Bill Luce, Jason Anderson, and Cory Hibbard.

For encouragement, coaching, and expertise in this new author world: Kevin Daum, TAE International; Jennifer Geiger, Sound Check Management; and Julie Ganz, Skyhorse Publishing.

And for being the best and most supportive family in the world: my husband, Al Fialkovich; parents, Judy Trilli and Jeff Palmer; sisters, Jaclyn Palmer Poole and Jaime Palmer; and closest friends Kerry McConnell and Paige Eber.

FOREWORD

The End Is Really the Beginning

Imagine this: you're sitting in an entrepreneurs' forum meeting, discussing with fellow business owners the struggles of leading a small company. One member gets an enormous smile on their face and says, "Well, I've actually done it. I've sold my company." Your jaw just about hits the floor, and you look around the room at the wide eyes of the others in the group. No one can believe they actually pulled the trigger. And you're happy for your colleague. Really, you are! But you're simultaneously struck with a tidal wave of jealousy.

While participating in Entrepreneurs' Organization (EO) and working with YPO (formerly Young Presidents' Organization), I noticed a certain look other entrepreneurs get when they hear an owner has sold their company. It's an expression of huge admiration, mixed in with frustration—even envy—that they haven't yet sold their own company.

It's not necessarily the financial windfall that inspires this jealousy. What's really enticing is the idea that the former owner now gets to begin a whole new journey. The newly-freed entrepreneur has the opportunity to reinvent themselves, start another company, or pursue other passions. And now they have the benefit of all the wisdom they gained in growing their former company.

You see, selling your company is not the end—it's a new beginning. And if there's something entrepreneurs love, it's beginnings!

My perspective on owning a business matches the common saying about owning a boat: the second happiest day of a business owner's life is the day their entrepreneurial dream becomes a reality and they start their company. The happiest day of their life is the day they move on from it.

The excitement of pending rebirth can motivate an owner to move too fast, focus less attention, and ultimately make mistakes in selling their company. Selling your business is a process that requires care and respect. This book is a remedy against those mistakes. Jessica has shared the benefit of her experience over thousands of transactions so you can move quickly, efficiently, and purposefully towards your exit.

I've exited companies in just about every way you can, some with a celebration and some with a boot in the ass. If you do it right—if you do as Jessica instructs—selling your company can earn you the freedom to move on to your next adventure, with none of the burdens of the past but all of the benefits.

We all want to get to closing day when you get the check and sail off into the sunset. But you need the information in this book to guide you through every step and to get you there in the best shape possible, without old strings holding you back. Many of you will skim this book, and that's fine. Use it to get a sense of the full process so you can see the entire picture, then use it as a reference as often as you need. Remember that the more diligent you are in preparing for sale, the cleaner your exit will be from this company, and the more freedom you'll have to start the next adventure.

Enjoy the ride—this one and the one to come!

—Kevin Daum

Introduction

As we packed our bags that morning, I looked at my husband, Al, and I knew. I said, "We have to sell the business." Even just a few months earlier, those words would have been unthinkable to both of us. That morning, however, Al nodded in agreement. It was the right decision.

We'd gotten to that place after the same journey many entrepreneurs take. Al and I each had corporate careers that lasted only a few years, but in that time, we saw more than enough. Al comes from an entrepreneurial family, so for him, the decision to go into business was a more natural one. For me, however, it flew in the face of everything I'd been taught. Although my grandfather ran a chain of pharmacies, my parents believed strongly in the stability of the forty-hour-a-week job and employer-matched 401(k) plans. By the time the 2008 financial crisis hit, however, I understood that the security I'd sought was a myth. The corporate overlords at the company Al and I worked at had just reduced the staff by 50 percent, and we knew we were headed for the same fate. My husband and I needed to rely on ourselves and create our own future.

We came up with all kinds of business ideas, ranging from a marketing firm to an online diet and exercise tracking service. Searching for inspiration, we walked into our favorite wine shop in Aspen, Colorado, where we were living. Grape and Grain was our home away from home, our Cheers. The store was outfitted with the best boutique wines you've never heard of, and somehow they understood and tracked the nuances of every one of their regular customers' palates. That day, we splurged on an expensive bottle of

Burgundy. On our walk back home, Al and I chatted about what a great gig it must be to run a store like that. They drank fancy wines, interacted with cool people, delivered a product that made people happy, and made a good living. The lightbulb went off. After one conversation with our friends at Grape and Grain, we knew what our business would be.

Al and I set off on a road trip down the west coast, tasting our way through Washington, Oregon, and California, to build our palates and plan our company. Considering we didn't know much about wine beyond the fact that we liked it, we had a lot to learn. Soon, we were in Naples, Florida, ready to start our new wine store, Decanted.

We did just about everything you aren't supposed to do when starting a business. We drained our meager retirement accounts, took advances on credit cards, and borrowed from family and friends. We refused to hire a contractor to build out the space we rented, determined to do it ourselves. By day, we were becoming wine experts, able to talk tannins, varietals, and more. But by night, we were becoming carpenters.

We made racks and shelves from scratch, sanding and staining every board. We constructed walls, installed plumbing, and built a bar. We learned how to resin countertops that featured old wine boxes and labels, still my favorite part of the store. After three months of preparation, we opened on December 11, 2009. If you'd told me that day that I would walk away from the store less than three years later, I never would have believed you. Decanted was, quite literally, born of our blood, sweat, and tears. It was a true labor of love—it was our baby.

Nothing could have persuaded me to sell the company that day, or most of the days that followed. The first year was hard—perhaps one of the hardest things I've ever done. We were managing tight cash flow, still operating on a minimal budget but trying to keep up with the market demand. Just as we started to get into a groove, we were dealt another blow—the BP Oil spill of 2010. Although Naples was better protected than most areas, tourism dipped and we quickly realized that we couldn't rely only on tourist season to keep our business profitable. We found our niche by developing an online presence and working with high-end collectors in the US, Canada, and Hong Kong. Our cash flow improved, we broke $1 million in revenue, and just kept growing. It was exhilarating.

It was also exhausting. Growth is great, but as many of you know, triple-digit growth can kill you. By 2012, we had achieved numbers we never thought possible. But working retail hours, plus connecting with collectors in multiple time zones on several continents, began to take its toll. One day I fell apart over—of all things—blow-drying my hair. I was exhausted and irritable after a late night, and from the car on the way to work, I called my mom, bawling my eyes out that I hadn't had a chance to blow-dry my hair that morning. Recognizing that my meltdown had nothing at all to do with my hair, my mom said, in her calm wisdom, "Honey, maybe this is just too much."

Shortly after that call, Al and I decided it was time to take our first real vacation since opening the store. We went back to Aspen, our happy place, and enjoyed five days of perfect powder, great restaurants, and reconnecting with friends and family. By the end of our stay, I finally had perspective. I was burning out. I didn't like retail, and I hated the hours. I missed Colorado. Worst of all, I was starting not to like the wine anymore! The last morning in town was when I told Al we needed to sell the company.

If you're a business reader, you know there is no shortage of resources to teach you how to start a business. There's plenty on how to grow a company, market a product, and develop yourself as a sales professional. You could spend a lifetime just reading the books, not to mention the academic courses, online tutorials, and how-to-videos also available. But if you want to sell a business, good luck, because you're on your own.

The truth is that entrepreneurs are only educated on two parts of the entrepreneurial journey: starting and growing. That journey, however, has a third part: exiting. And exit you will, one way or another. Perhaps you'll leave by choice, perhaps you'll be forced out, or perhaps you'll be carried out feet first. Whatever the method, one day it will be gone from your life.

Despite the inevitability of exiting, there's almost nothing out there to guide owners on how to approach this incredibly important process. Sure, if I had a $50 million company, there would be people knocking down my door to help me sell it. But where is the guidance for business owners with $10 million in revenue? $5 million? Even $500,000? Ninety-six percent of US companies never achieve $1 million in annual revenue. How could such a vast majority be so woefully under-served?

How were Al and I supposed to go about selling our company? It was a successful but niche wine business, with rapidly-developing online competition, in a small city. Would anyone want to buy it? If so, how would we find them? What would they pay? When I reached out to our business advisors, no one had an answer.

I'd ignored the warning signs pointing toward exit for so long that I was totally unprepared for the sales process, and had nothing left in me to put towards it. As a result, we skipped all the prep work we should have done and took the company straight to market. We hired the only business broker in town, blindly accepting his valuation and advice (some of which I now know was incorrect). Our broker was able to secure three potential buyers, but basically abandoned us after that. We were left to navigate due diligence, negotiation, deal structuring, and closing on our own, with only a lawyer supporting us. On the day of closing, we signed some paperwork at our lawyer's office and had some champagne. Our business broker, who had totally disappeared on us for ninety days, arrived to collect his largely-undeserved commission check—and then tried to sell me life insurance.

Looking back, Al and I were very, very lucky. So many things could have gone wrong. If our books hadn't already been in order, I might not have had the patience to fix them. If the buyer hadn't been so relaxed, she might have negotiated harder on any number of items or demanded a longer transition period. Heck, if I'd had more energy, I might have fought the business broker for being so unhelpful. No entrepreneur should have to go through the sales process so blindly and so reliant on luck, particularly when that business is something they love (or at least, loved!) so deeply.

After selling my company, I couldn't shake how close we had come to failure. The entrepreneurial juices were flowing again. I had sold my first baby in Decanted, but I was ready to raise another: I was determined to save other business owners from the sales pitfalls that so easily could have befallen us. Over 99 percent of US companies are classified as small businesses, yet they are often treated as the annoying younger sibling with nothing to offer until (or if) they grow up.

Our experience is why Al and I started the Colorado location of Transworld Business Advisors, and then expanded to Dallas/Fort Worth and Las Vegas. American small businesses need a brokerage and exit strategy firm that provides expert guidance to meet their unique needs. No one should go through the sales process alone. My Transworld offices have been recognized by the International Business Brokers Association as doing the largest number of deals of any brokerage in the country, and ours is the number-one Transworld location in the world. As we've helped close hundreds of deals every year, Al and I have realized how much money sellers leave on the table. Due to a lack of basic preparation, many owners sell their companies for far less than they are worth—if they can sell at all. When we introduced our Prep to Sell program in 2018, our goal was simple: to reveal behind-the-scenes knowledge that would allow owners to increase both the value of their companies and the likelihood of sale.

My goal is the same with this book. The best way to use it is as an introductory guide to the sales process. I cover each step in the process, what to expect, and how to proceed effectively through each stage. Look, I know you're busy running your company and barely have time for anything else. It would be great if you can read this book from cover to cover and absorb the overall picture of the sales process. If you can't, that's okay—use this book as a reference. Find what you need in the table of contents, and return to the text as often as you need. I've given you shortcuts with the key takeaways and to-do lists at the end of chapters 1 through 5. I've also provided several top ten lists in chapters 6 through 10, as well as a glossary of terms and a resource guide. All the business stories I share in this book are based on real world scenarios I've encountered, although some details have been changed to protect confidentiality.

I know there are much more urgent things going on in your business and your life. But the single most important action you can take in your business is to start preparing for your exit now. It may not happen tomorrow, next month, or even in two years, but it will happen, and typically much sooner than you planned. Starting your preparation now will allow you to sleep better at night and to enjoy the process of exiting when that day comes.

CHAPTER 1

Strategy on Selling

HOW COULD I POSSIBLY SELL MY BABY?

Most of my brokerage's business owner clients fall into one of two buckets. If you're in the first group, you can hardly believe you're considering selling your business. Until recently, it was unimaginable to you. You've poured your blood, sweat, and tears into it. It's consumed your time and maybe even your identity. But just like I did with my companies, you've decided you're ready to move on to something else. It can be a difficult, emotional decision that can feel like walking away from a beloved child.

If you're in the second group of owners, your business has become an insolent teenager who does what it wants and doesn't listen to a thing you say anymore. Your life has become about serving a business baby that has no empathy for your needs. You take a long weekend for the first time in what feels like years. And BOOM! You're barely gone for a few hours before your manager quits, the HVAC system goes out, the website crashes, or a top client doesn't receive their order. You spend the entire "vacation" solving problems remotely, only to come home even more exhausted than when you left. It's time for someone else to take on the burden. It's time for your business baby to fly the coop, and it can't happen soon enough.

Either of these situations can feel overwhelming—even paralyzing—for the owner. Realize that you're going to exit the company one day, whether by force or by choice. You've taken the first step in deciding to move on, and that was hard enough. Unfortunately, there's still much to be done. You need to lead the charge to an outcome that will bring you maximum value and create the best result for your company. All this takes preparation and hard work, but the results are well worth it.

THE BEST LAID PLANS . . .

Life, and the humans in it, are unpredictable and uncontrollable. In fact, many of the most unpredictable and uncontrollable people I know are entrepreneurs (it takes one to know one, right?). Many entrepreneurs—including me—thought we'd never, ever sell our business, or assumed it was so far in the future that it wasn't worth considering. It's a nice thought, but ultimately, you don't get to make that decision. All entrepreneurs leave their businesses, either walking out the front door head held high, or being carried out feet first.

You Need Exit Options, Not an Exit Plan (Yet)

Most business brokers will tell you that you need to design an exit plan right now. An exit plan is a definite decision about how you will exit the company, what you'll get out of it, and when it will happen. Some less scrupulous brokers will happily take a bunch of your money to put together a beautifully bound, 100-page exit plan booklet explaining how it'll all happen—and it's a work of complete fiction. I'm here to tell you that you don't need an exit plan, at least right now. What you need are exit *options*, which are strategies designed in advance that provide a long-term path to success, while also preparing you in case of the need for a quick exit (more on this later in the chapter).

For small to medium businesses, there are only four possible outcomes that you can choose (assuming you don't choose to get carried out feet first):

1. You milk the company for all the cash it's worth, and board up and walk away when you're done.

2. You sell the business to a third party.
3. You sell the business to a key employee.
4. You transition the company to a family member or business partner.

Unless you're looking to exit as soon as possible, you don't necessarily need to select right now which outcome is your preferred choice. You should, however, be prepared for any of these four possibilities. That way, if something unexpected arises, you're ready to tackle it without having to scramble.

Hopefully, one day long in the future, you will make a definite exit plan. But until that day comes, you need to arm yourself with exit options. Don't put it off. I can't tell you how many clients I've worked with who say they'll work on exit options in a year or two, and come to regret it.

HOW DO I FIND A BUYER?

One of the most frequent questions from business sellers is how they will find their buyer. There's no such thing as newspaper classified ads or open houses where potential buyers can see what businesses are on the market. Should owners put a sign in the window? Advertise online? Are there other methods they don't know about? I even heard of a business owner who tried to give away his company to a college student in exchange for some future royalties—although I don't recommend this tactic.

One source of buyers is through your existing industry connections. In a tight-knit industry or one where mergers and acquisitions (M&A) are popular, such as the wealth management space, owners can find buyers through their network, including using reverse cold-calling or getting introduced through a mutual acquaintance.

There are direct marketing options for owners determined to do it themselves, but you're taking a major risk if you go this route. You can advertise on business sales websites and cold call potential buyers. It can get the job done, but it loses the biggest group of potential purchasers: the individual buyers, who usually go to brokers and bankers first.

Get a Business Broker

You may be tempted to think you can find a buyer on your own, but don't be so sure. Most owners know a lot about running their company, but almost nothing about selling it. The best way to find buyers is through business brokers or investment bankers. If your company is worth less than $25 million (more on valuation later in this chapter), you're likely to use a broker. If it's over $25 million, you'll probably use an investment banker. Both accomplish the same goal: finding the right buyer and selling the business. They create competition for your deal by using confidential advertising and marketing strategies sellers usually can't create on their own. In many cases, brokers can create a market for the company that wouldn't exist without them.

There is a big difference between finding a buyer and getting a deal done. At least half of all deals fall apart after a buyer is identified, and owners without experience in buying and selling businesses can stumble in this area. The owners of a medical company reached out to our brokerage in desperation. The owners had been trying to sell it themselves, and had even gotten a few nibbles, but couldn't get a deal done. They'd had it on the market for four years; as soon as they hired our business brokerage, the company sold within four months at a price 50 percent higher than the owners expected.

Buyers also treat sellers without brokers differently. Some will take advantage of the situation. Knowing there is no one who's particularly deal-savvy involved in the transaction, they'll try to underprice their offer or insert nefarious deal terms that can create a nightmare for former owners down the road. Other buyers are wary of buying businesses that don't have third-party representation, and assume the company is somehow of a lower quality. A broker can help both sides feel confident the sale is being negotiated under standard market terms. Perhaps most importantly, a broker knows how to market your company confidentially. If employees and customers find out you're selling, there's a huge risk that they'll leave, and you'll be left with nothing at all to sell.

SO, WHO ARE THESE MYTHICAL BUSINESS BUYERS?

Most business owners looking to sell think of buyers as either larger companies or private equity firms. There's something romantic about a group of deep-pocketed experts recognizing the hidden gem that is your life's work. In reality, those buyers are the minority. Whoever or whatever buys your business, you want to find your "most probable buyer"—the one who will pay the most, be the easiest to make a deal with, and provide the best legacy for your company.

There are a variety of entities looking to buy companies:

- **Individuals**—These are typically business veterans who have worked extensively in the corporate world. They've always dreamed of owning their own business, and have decided buying is a better strategy than starting one themselves. Individuals make up about 80 percent of business buyers. Many sellers, lost in their daydream of a private equity firm dumping a truckload of cash on their front lawn, totally ignore this group of buyers at first. Do this at your peril: it's highly likely that your buyer will be one of these individuals, and that they'll provide you with a better deal than any alternative.
- **Strategic / Synergistic**—These buyers are businesses that are either a direct competitor or in a similar enough industry that combining with your company will increase its growth factor. Many times, they come from a different region or market and are looking to expand into yours. These companies are generally just a bit larger than yours—usually 25 to 75 percent larger. Put away the notion that a large, billion-dollar company is going to acquire your $1 to $2 million revenue

business. Multinational firms have huge M&A divisions, and it takes a much more sizable EBITDA (earnings before interest, taxes, depreciation, and amortization—more on this later in the chapter) for them to even give you a sniff.

- **Private Equity**—PE groups are collections of investors looking to buy a business, grow it over three to seven years, and then sell it for a premium. They're typically only interested in companies with EBITDAs of more than $1 million per year. Considering only 4 percent of US companies even achieve *revenue* of more than $1 million per year, these buyers are looking at less than 1 percent of the market. Plus, they're very particular about elements like industry, growth prospects, owner's role, and people in the organization. PE firms are likely to offer deal structures that shift the risk back onto the seller, and often try to change terms close to closing. Generally, PE deals are bad for sellers.
- **Flippers**—Yes, they exist, and yes, they're similar to house flippers. These buyers are looking for a company where they can add value with their individual skill sets and then sell in one to three years. These buyers typically don't pay the most, but they move quickly and can be great for sellers who appreciate speed. Flippers are also willing to put in the hard work to turn around struggling companies and may be ideal for sellers in sticky situations.
- **Internal**—You can also sell your business to someone who already exists in your world. It may be your general manager, your child, or a business partner. These buyers are great for the legacy of the company because they already understand the company ethos. The deal can present financial challenges if the buyer can't come up with an adequate down payment or qualify for full financing, which can also lengthen the process. This type of sale can also involve additional emotional factors that can complicate the process.

Even successful sellers usually have only a small handful of bidders. And that's okay! The best buyer, after all, is the one you can get to the closing table. Find as many potential buyers as possible and rank them by your preferred method of transaction. Remember, increasing the number of possible buyers increases competition for your sale. This improves the likelihood that your company will sell, and increases the price you'll get for it.

WHY WOULD ANYONE WANT MY BUSINESS?

The first time you thought about selling your business, the first question that probably popped in your mind was, *What's my business even worth?* Unfortunately, there's no simple answer. Despite what the internet told you—shocking, I know—there's no single surefire way for most people to value a business. It's part art and part science. No matter how many rules of thumb you apply, online calculators (even ours!) you reference, or "industry experts" you consult, it's hard to predict what a willing buyer and willing seller will agree is a fair price in neutral market conditions. Ultimately, you won't get an accurate valuation until you go to a business broker and put your company on the market. And up until that point, most owners live in a fantasy world when they think about the value of their company, assuming it's either worthless or priceless.

Your Baby Isn't That Ugly . . .

Some owners think they have the ugliest, most foul-mouthed child on the planet, and are certain no one else would want to run it, let alone pay for the privilege. Chances are that these owners are wrong. Just like parents with unruly children, owners are often too close to the company to separate the bad times from the good and see all they've accomplished.

Almost all companies have some value that will attract buyers. It's just a matter of identifying the thing(s) of value, understanding the likely buyer, and determining what they're willing to pay for it.

You may walk away with only $10,000 instead of the $10 million you were hoping for, but unlocking that value is still better than shutting the doors and walking away.

. . . But It Isn't That Gorgeous Either

Other owners think they have a golden child, a company that is beautiful in every way and can do no wrong. Its value is outweighed only by its potential! Surely any buyer would jump at the chance to buy this once-in-a-lifetime company! And indeed, maybe you are sitting on the next Facebook. But it's far more likely you've built a functional business that has both upside and challenges.

Selling your company is possible, but your baby probably needs an honest evaluation of its merits and shortcomings and some sprucing up to be attractive to buyers and fetch you the price you dream of. This may hurt, but better to rip off the bandage up front: Your company is likely not worth as much as you think or hope it is. Your dedication and passion are commendable, but they don't translate into more zeroes in an offer.

Wherever you fall on the spectrum, relax. The truth is likely somewhere in the middle. Following the steps in this book will help you get the most value possible from your company.

But My CPA Said!

If your CPA (or any advisor other than your business broker) comes up with an astronomical valuation for your company, tell them you're willing to sell it to them at that price today! They'll politely decline, and you should go get a second opinion.

When trying to figure out what your business is worth, lots of people claim to have the magic formula for you. I've already discussed the inaccuracy of the internet, but hiring the wrong advisor to do a valuation can be equally troublesome. The advisor you select to give you a valuation should always be involved in the business sale marketplace. It gives them access to private sale data (which they'll use in comps—more on those below) and puts them in regular contact with buyers and banks so they understand the market realities that impact price. These advisors will also know to use the market valuation method (again, more below), which is what buyers and banks use. Other advisors may claim to have fancy, Ivy League-sounding tools and methods that look great on a chart, but these don't translate into realistic numbers. Finally, beware of anyone who wants to charge more than a few thousand dollars for a valuation.

By the end of this book, you'll have heard this piece of advice about a million times: you should get a business broker.

OK, SO WHAT *IS* MY BUSINESS WORTH?

Owners need to understand how businesses values are calculated, and unfortunately, there's a great deal of bad information out there about valuation. Business brokers are particularly useful here because they can evaluate all the factors that determine a valuation and give you a realistic number. A beauty products manufacturer was looking to sell his company and had a valuation done by an industry expert—but one who wasn't familiar with buying and selling small businesses. The expert assigned a multi-million-dollar valuation based on elements like the company's Instagram audience engagement. The company's profits, however, didn't support this valuation, and when the owner began working with a broker, he was disappointed to learn his company actually was worth about $500,000.

Remember that that even business brokers are making a prediction. The valuation they assign is a baseline, or a starting point from which to begin your prep-to-sell journey. The more you can get an accurate—and conservative—understanding of the value of your business, the more ability you will have to put in place strategies to increase that value. By the time you actually take the company to market, you'll have had opportunities to nudge the valuation needle up, up, up.

Lions and Numbers and Jargon . . . Oh My!

While there are a number of ways to value a business (including asset valuation, discounted cash flow valuation, and more), we'll focus on the most common method for small businesses: market valuation. In this method, potential buyers determine the multiple they're willing to pay, and then apply that multiple to an earnings number. We'll get to multiples in a minute. Let's tackle the earnings number first.

Let's kill one common myth right away: Your revenue is *not* your earnings number. In fact, revenue may have very little bearing on earnings. One company with $1 million in revenue may make a profit of $250,000, while another company with the same revenue may make a profit of only $25,000. Obviously, these companies will not command the same sales price. Similarly, a company with $800,000 in revenue and 50 percent margins makes more money than a company with $3 million in revenue and 10 percent margins.

For buyers, cash and return on investment trump all. Therefore, they're mostly concerned with the earnings number—which means you should be, too. For larger companies, the earnings number used is EBITDA (earnings before interest, taxes, depreciation, and amortization). For smaller companies, the earnings number is SDE, or seller's discretionary earnings. SDE, also known as cash flow, is EBITDA plus one working owner's annual pay and benefits. Basically, SDE is how much monetary benefit an owner is receiving from the activities of the business. SDE is a useful number because it allows every company, no matter size or industry, to be compared on an even playing field.

SDE vs. EBITDA

So which earnings number should you use? Many times, it's irrelevant, and the more important decision is making sure you match the proper multiple. Still, the difference between the two is useful to understand. The earnings number used depends on the size of the business; generally, smaller companies use SDE, while larger companies use EBITDA.

Stay with me here: A company's SDE will be higher than its EBITDA, since SDE includes the owner's salary. Therefore, SDE multiples are lower, since the earnings number they're assigned to is higher. Below is a chart illustrating the difference between an SDE and EBITDA valuation for the same company. The value is the same, but the numbers to get there are different.

Sample Company Valuation, Compared		
	EBITDA	**SDE**
Earnings Number	$315,000	$490,000
Multiple	4.2	2.7
Business Value	$1,323,000	$1,323,000

Again, smaller companies usually use SDE. Based on SDE, the average multiple across the past ten years of business sales under $10 million is 2.4. If you're doing the rough math in your head and are disappointed with what you calculate, you're not alone. Later in this chapter, you'll learn that with the exception of private equity groups, all buyers are human beings just like you. They want to buy a business that will generate a reasonable income to take care of their families.

What's a Multiple?

You can see in the chart above the multiples applied to each earnings number. But where did 4.2 and 2.7 come from? Did I conjure them out of thin air? Well, sort of, but not really. I told you it was complicated!

Once your broker determines the earnings number to use, they'll search for comps: sales of companies that are similar to yours based on size, location, and industry. They'll determine the earnings numbers and multiples applied in those sales (brokers have access to these numbers, while many others do not), and approximate what kind of multiple might be applied in your case. If comparable sales received multiples between 2x and 4x SDE, what makes your company closer to one instead of the other?

Like the earnings number, the multiple used depends on the circumstances. The multiple is a function of both the quantitative earnings of the business and the qualitative factors of how well the company is being run and how much growth potential it has. You can think of a multiple as the amount of risk the buyer is accepting. Smaller companies with less profit and less infrastructure have more risk, so their multiples will be lower; larger companies, which have more room for error by a new owner, get higher multiples.

This is good news for owners: Increasing the valuation of your business doesn't rely only on growth and profit exclusively, but also on efficiency and potential. Chapters 3, 4, and 5 will cover strategies that impact all of these elements.

Don't Lose Money to Your Ego

When you sell your company, you want to walk away with as much cold, hard cash as possible. As you'll see in Chapter 10, some sellers mistakenly worry more about valuation than they do about sale price. High valuations sound nice, but you can't pay your bills with them. It's all theory until you agree on a sale price and the amount of cash at closing—what the buyer will actually pay you. That's money you can spend.

Now, just because your company is reasonably valued at a certain number doesn't mean an offer will match it dollar for dollar. Owners sometimes balk unnecessarily when the price they're offered doesn't match the valuation. In reality, there are times when a lower valuation actually is *better* for the seller. Here's an example:

An owner was selling her consulting company and had two offers. The first buyer assigned a lower valuation of $1.5 million to the company, but the owner would receive 100 percent of the price up front via bank financing. The second buyer assigned a valuation of $3 million, but the owner would receive only $1 million up front. The rest could be earned via earnout if she led the company to $5 million in revenue after two years. Excited by the impressive $3 million valuation, the seller accepted the second buyer's offer. By the end of the two years, she reached $4.9 million in revenue. It was huge growth, but she missed the earnout. If she had accepted the lower valuation, she would have received $500,000 more and saved two years of her life.

SHOW ME THE MONEY

So you've decided to sell your company, you know what the business is worth, you've found a buyer, and you are closing the deal. You know how you "paid" for your company: with years of blood, sweat, tears, and sacrifice. So now the question is, how will a buyer pay for it?

In an ideal world, the perfect buyer will appear with a huge stack of cash and the belief they've just found the Next Big Thing in your company. Reality is a bit more nuanced. No matter the type of buyer, there are four basic methods of financing the purchase. While any one of them could account for the entire sale, it's highly likely your deal will involve a combination of several.

In order of what most sellers prefer, the types of payment methods are:

- **Cash**—In cash transactions, the buyer pays up front with their own cash. (Almost no buyer offers a full 100 percent of the price in cash up front. Even if they're truly using all cash, they keep some percentage of the sale price until after the transition period to make sure the seller has incentive to help if necessary. The only exception is when the seller is desperate to get out ASAP, and this often means accepting a lower price than what the company is actually worth.) Even if it's not a total cash transaction, you still need to be aware of how much cash your buyer can bring to the table, as it will impact how they finance the rest of the deal and how much money they have to run the business after closing. At a minimum, your buyer should have at least 10 percent of the purchase price in cash.

- **SBA or Bank Financing**—Most buyers get a loan backed by the Small Business Administration (SBA). In some rare cases, a buyer may be able to secure a conventional bank loan. Whatever the loan type, most banks allow a buyer to borrow up to 80 percent of the price, meaning the buyer needs at least 20 percent in cash. Banks also often require some seller financing (percentages may differ) to ensure the seller helps create a smooth transition. Typically, the 20 percent down payment to the bank consists of 10 percent cash from the buyer and 10 percent financing from the seller.
- **Seller Financing**—You, the seller, act as the bank and loan the buyer the money for a certain period of time at an agreed-upon interest rate. These transactions often are pursued not because the buyer can't secure the financing, but rather because the buyer wants the seller to have skin in the game and assist with the transition. It's also a great way for a seller to have deferred income with a good yield.
- **Earnouts**—Here, the seller receives some money up front, but later also receives a larger chunk of the purchase price based on future activities of the company. That chunk may be a share of the revenue, profit, or some other metric defined in the sales agreement. These structures can be good for both parties, but there are downsides. If the seller leaves the company altogether, they lose all control of whether the goal metric is achieved. If the seller stays on in some capacity, they still may not be able to influence the company's outcomes as much as they once were. In either case, the earnout is usually an all-or-nothing proposition: if the company misses the goal by even a tiny amount, the seller gets none of the remaining chunk of money. This structure is used most often by PE groups, but also can be useful in rapid-growth or -decline companies that are difficult to valuate. My brokerage advises sellers to use revenue as the metric of choice, as profit can be easily manipulated.

The more you're open to the four different options, the more potential buyers you'll have. This will increase competition for your company and thereby its price. A willingness to be flexible on financing method may also help you improve the deal. And remember, most transactions involve multiple payment methods.

TIMING THE MARKET IS A MYTH

Stockbrokers love to wax poetic about timing the market when buying and selling stocks. You may assume the same is true in buying and selling businesses, but it doesn't hold true. Year to year, small business sales are steady over time. If you average the multiples at which businesses have sold for the last twenty to thirty years, the numbers are stable. The good news for you is that it's almost always a seller's market. At any given time, in any industry, there are tons of buyers: generally a ratio of twenty to fifty buyers for every seller. The bad news is that only about 20 percent of listed businesses actually sell, no matter how much their owners love them and think they're invaluable. This is largely because the owners don't prepare and don't understand how the business market works, not because they've timed the market wrong. There are lots of ways to increase the likelihood of selling your company, but timing the market isn't one of them.

Now, even though you can't time the market generally, there still are right and wrong times to sell your business. Growth potential is one of the most important things a buyer looks for. The business cycle has four phases: startup, growth, peak, and decline. You should try to time your sale on an upswing, but never at a peak; buyers want to purchase when there's still room for growth. Timing within the calendar year can be critical, too, particularly in industries that experience seasonality in activity and revenue. Buyers prefer to purchase these types of businesses during the company's offseason. Buyers then have time to learn the business and adjust to their new life before the insanity of the busy season kicks off.

When Is Right for Me?

Some business owners feel financial pressure to sell because they've received an offer or because of market conditions. Most of the time, however, selling a business is more about how the owner wants to spend their time, and less about finances. If you still enjoy the work and are making good money, it's usually a better financial decision to keep running the company. Owners usually sell because they want to do something different with their time, such as retire, start a new company, etc., in spite of the fiscal ramifications. Understandably, it can be quite emotional.

There are other personal reasons why an owner may want or need to sell a business right away—or discover that selling isn't the right move. You need to put thought into what you're going to do next. After undergoing the valuation process, some who are considering selling find it simply isn't financially prudent to sell. Often, however, life gets in the way, and personal situations require an immediate exit. These may include burnout, health events, or even death. It's incredibly important to be prepared with exit options so you can be nimble in case of an emergency.

An owner built a highly successful construction company. He became a very wealthy man, but his work required him to be absent for much of the childhoods of his three kids. He frequently missed soccer games, birthday parties, and even family vacations. When his kids got married and started having children of their own, he decided not to miss any more time with his family. He sold his company despite the fact that it was still growing and bringing him a great deal of money. Sellers such as these, who have decided to move on but are not strapped for time, can strategize and prepare for the most beneficial exit situation.

Unfortunately, other owners sell for more traumatic, time-sensitive reasons. One man worked for years developing a chemical company. He was successful, but the long hours and years of stress led to a number of serious health problems. He hadn't planned to sell for several years, but with his health declining, he was forced to sell as soon as possible. Another couple owned an electronics company, but a death in the family rendered them emotionally unable to continue running the business. Sellers in these situations are forced to sell quickly, often at a lower price and with riskier deal structures. If they'd had exit options in place, they would have been better able to manage the process of walking away.

These are depressing stories, but they highlight an important point. We're discussing the *best* time to sell your company, but the reality is that you need to be prepared to sell your company on a moment's notice. You simply don't know what's going to happen in your life, so you need "In Case of Emergency" exit strategies. Happily, the more you're able to follow the steps in this book, the better prepared you'll be for any situation. You should run your business as if it's always for sale. It will help you run a better business, and help you sleep easier at night.

WHAT'S NEXT?

Once you understand the basics of the business sales process and come to terms with the reality of your company's value, you can begin gathering the team you'll need to align your resources for the sale. And if you aren't happy with the valuation, there are ways you can increase it in as little as six months. More on that in Chapter 8.

KEY TAKEAWAYS:

- You don't need to worry about an exit plan yet, but you need exit options now. If something happens to you or the business, you need to know you can exit no matter the circumstance.
- There are many buyer types. Don't focus on just large companies and private equity firms.
- All companies have value. It's just a matter of what that value is and who will buy it.
- Business valuation is part art, part science, and best handled by a professional—not the internet.

TO DO NOW:

- Have a business transactions professional do a valuation on your company. Learn more at exitfactor.com/valuations.
- Meet with an exit strategist to help define exit options for your business. Also itemize the elements within your company that are sellable even if you can't sell the whole business.

CHAPTER 2

Mastering the Process

ESTABLISHING THE TIMELINE

When selling your company, you need to begin with the end in mind. Selling a business is a process that takes time. For all deals across all industries, the average amount of time between the day you list your company for sale and the day you close the deal is eight to nine months. And remember, your preparatory work started long before you listed the company. If you own a business in a narrow niche industry or in a rural area, you may have to add one to two years to the process. Ultimately it's about how wide your buyer pool is. Looking for a needle in a haystack naturally will take longer. A tourism-based company in a rural area may take twenty-four months to sell, while the same business in a city may hold closer to the national average of eight and a half months.

Understand that selling a business is not like buying and selling stock. In the stock market, you time your sales and purchases based on what you believe will maximize your outcomes. A few weeks—heck, even a few hours—can make a huge difference in your profits and losses. But this idea of "timing the market" doesn't really apply to buying and selling businesses. The business sales market is remarkably stable over time, so the status of the market isn't likely to make a huge difference. (Of course there are exceptions to this rule when there are dramatic market changes, like the 2008 financial crisis or COVID-19.)

While you can't "time the market," this isn't to say timing isn't important. In fact, it's critical. But the timing that matters is centered around your company and your industry. You need to consider where your company is in its business lifecycle. Is it on the way up? At its peak? On the way down? The ability to demonstrate both recent growth and the potential for future growth will impact your ability to sell and the price you get. You also must understand how the calendar year impacts your business. It's usually better to sell during a quieter time of year. It may sound counterintuitive at first—wouldn't you want to wait until peak season, so you can get the highest price?—but buyers understand annual cycles, and they're more likely to buy when they'll have some time to adjust to running the business before the busy season starts.

In the end, all that matters is ending up on a beach with a bottle of *very* expensive champagne. So, what is the day you want to be there? You should start planning at least twelve, and preferably twenty-four, months in advance of that date. There are considerable advantages to long preparation. In addition to maximizing time factors, it also allows you the opportunity to position your company financially to achieve the best price possible. You'll have time to understand the value of your business and overcome obstacles. (Chapters 3, 4, and 5 cover the main value drivers and deal killers that can make or break your deal.) Of course, some owners have no choice; for any number of reasons, they may be forced to sell as soon as possible. But if you have control over the timing, I suggest you give yourself at least twelve months to prepare your company for sale, and then another twelve months to actually close the deal.

Speed Bumps

It takes long enough to prepare a company for sale. And even if you find a buyer, half of all deals die in due diligence. To avoid unnecessary delays, sellers need to understand the risks of waiting too long and what can hold up a deal. Having a five- to ten-year exit strategy is fine, and is certainly something you should discuss with your financial advisor. But in terms of selling your business, twelve to twenty-four months is optimal. Long delays can mean markets and buyer preferences can change. No seller I've ever known has regretted selling, but many have regretted not selling sooner.

Delays can be deadly. A family printing company was involved in manufacturing postal scales, printing for marketing campaigns, and postage sales. The owner developed a long-term exit strategy involving her children, but she came to learn they did not want to continue the business. In the time between designing her exit plan and realizing her children were not interested, postage sales and direct-mail marketing plummeted. It was basically impossible to sell the company. Instead, the owner had to delay retirement and acquire a company in digital marketing. It wasn't until several years later and a lot of hard work that she was able to nurture the company back to health and consider selling again.

In another case, the owner of a professional services business was considering selling his company. The company had been stable for thirty years, and he wasn't sure it was the right time to sell. He thought he might hang on for another year or two of profitability. Eventually he decided to move forward with a good offer from a very enthusiastic buyer. A few months after closing, a new competitor entered the market and the buyer lost 90 percent of the business within three weeks. The buyer eventually recovered, but if the seller had waited even a couple months to sell, the value of his company would have plummeted, and it would have forced him to delay his sale by two to three years.

The buyer vetting process is also an important one. You don't want to get all the way to closing only to realize the buyer can't actually afford the purchase. When you and your broker are evaluating buyers, make sure you understand exactly what they're willing—and able—to pay. If financing is an element of the deal, the bank approval process takes time. See what you can find out about their relationship with the bank. Some buyers prefer to work with certain banks. This can be a good sign if it indicates they have a good relationship with their financing partner, especially if the buyer and bank have experience working together to buy companies.

But a buyer's relationship with a bank can also be a complicating factor. If the bank doesn't have experience with business sales or working with the SBA, it can wreak havoc on a deal. The sale of a janitorial business was supposed to close on December 15, but the buyer insisted on working with a particular bank. The bank wasn't equipped to handle the sale; they didn't have the right team or the process that comes with experience. The bank wasn't able to close the transaction until February 8. This was two additional months the seller waited in limbo, when he could have been sipping that champagne or working on a new venture. Worse still, the seller needed to sell the business in order to pay some personal debts, and the delay meant he came within days of needing to file for bankruptcy.

Perhaps one of the biggest potential holdups is your landlord. Surprisingly, most commercial real estate contracts give landlords an incredible amount of power to influence—or even outright kill—deals. Many give landlords full veto power over proposed assignments or subleases, even without providing a justification. You may think it wouldn't be a big deal to move office locations. That may be true, if you really only need generic office space and your employees are flexible. But leases often impose huge penalties for early termination. Further, if location is important to your company, as in retail, restaurants, or manufacturing, you may have an issue. Think about what a pain it is to move from one house to another; it's even more difficult to move your business to a new location, and it's just about the last thing a new buyer wants to deal with. And that's *if* you can get out of your current lease in the first place. Anecdotally, of the 50 percent of deals that die in due diligence, about half of those are death by landlord.

If you're thinking about selling, examine your lease right away. Determine how long it lasts, whether you have the ability to assign or sublet, and what options you have for renegotiation. The best thing you can do is protect yourself from pro-landlord clauses before you enter into any lease—just one more reason to have a good attorney. After the fact, the attorney and your broker can help you decide when to talk to the landlord, what to say, and how to manage any negotiations.

Sellers also need to recognize that their own desires will impact the speed at which they're able to sell. Brokers usually are able to determine valuations that match closely with what buyers end up paying. Ultimately, however, the business is worth what a buyer is willing to pay for it. If you have unrealistic expectations about what your company is worth and what you can demand from a buyer, your company will languish on the market. You need to be willing to adjust to what the market will bear, or you could wait forever.

Preparation Drives Deals

Delays can make the sales process feel interminable. In reality, a full preparation period is not always necessary. It is possible to sell a business without any preparation (indeed, some owners are forced to), and you can even do some great preparatory work in as little as six months. Chapter 8 provides a timeline-driven guide for how to pull this off. But the longer you give yourself, the more likely you are to sell your business, and for more money. Of all companies listed for sale, only about 20 percent sell in a given year. If you don't prepare well, you're far more likely to fall into the 80 percent that don't sell. And even if you are able to sell, you're likely to sell for less money and at a lower multiple.

Sometimes a company that once failed to sell can suddenly become a hot commodity after some basic prep work is completed. The owner of a property management company wanted to retire. His books were a mess, but the business was profitable and the industry desirable, so he went to market anyway—and got absolutely nowhere. It lingered on the market for months. Frustrated, the owner took it off the market and hired a controller to clean up the last three years of financial records. He didn't do anything different with the business or make any changes other than fixing the books. When he relisted the company, it sold for full price within three months.

In an ideal world, you'll have twenty-four months to prepare your company and get the best price possible. A heavy equipment rental company had been growing rapidly, and the team was hoping for a multi-million-dollar exit. The valuation put the company at around $650,000, which was disappointing. Wisely, they were planning eighteen months in advance and had plenty of time to make the business more attractive. Their broker helped them work through Exit Factor's Prep to Sell Process, where we guide owners as they systematically eliminate deal killers and solidify aspects of their business that increase value. During the preparation process, the owners realized a huge percentage of their business came from a single client, which is a risky proposition for a buyer. The owners used their prep time to diversify their customer base so the company was less reliant on a single source. When they finally did go to market twelve months later, they found a buyer and closed within six months. Better yet, they got over 80 percent more than their original valuation. That translated to more than double the cash in the pockets of each owner with just eighteen months of work. Think of all the extra champagne!

THE MECHANICS OF THE SALES PROCESS

In the Introduction, I discussed my disappointment that there are so few resources available for owners looking to sell their small businesses. There are a million books and blogs about building a company, but almost nothing about exiting it. Every single owner will exit their company one way or another, but most know little about it. If you're going to have a successful sale of your company, you need to understand how the process works. The sales process for small- to lower-mid-sized businesses has five parts:

1. Prepare for the Sale

The Players: You and your planning advisor (such as an exit strategist)

What Happens: You'll determine the baseline of your business value and define your goals for the sale. You'll work to eliminate deal killers from your business, develop elements in your operations to drive value, and set a timeline for going to market. You'll also establish your most probable buyer—the one who will pay an adequate price and ensure the continuity of your business. This is the bulk of what will be covered in Chapters 3, 4, and 5.

2. Go to Market

The Players: You and your broker

What Happens: This is when you hire your broker and perhaps your attorney. The broker will verify the valuation and confirm what the asking price will be. The broker will also put together a marketing strategy explaining how they plan to attract your most probable buyer. Then you're ready to list your company for sale! All businesses are marketed confidentially, although your broker may choose to reveal the industry. They may use business sales websites for mass marketing, or tap into their network for more targeted strategies.

3. Find and Qualify a Buyer

The Players: You, your broker, and the buyer

What Happens: In this stage, your broker will solicit interest from potential buyers using non-disclosure agreements, or NDAs. Potential buyers will undergo a qualification process where your broker confirms the buyer has the funds and the right intentions, and isn't just window shopping or trying to steal the recipe to your secret sauce. Qualification includes several steps, including an initial phone call, followed by two or three meetings between the broker and buyer, and later a meeting with the seller. Your broker tries to protect your time and the best interests of your company by bringing you only the most serious and qualified buyers. At this point, the buyer will also start (if they haven't already) working with the bank to determine financing.

4. Negotiate a Deal

The Players: You, your advisors, the buyer, and the buyer's advisors
What Happens: This stage is the longest and most complex. When the buyer makes an offer, it's time to start negotiating. Most buyers will make an offer that's close to your asking price. This is a short-term marriage where you'll work together very closely, so they recognize it's best to start off on the right foot and not piss you off with a lowball offer. Generally, potential buyers make a good offer, or no offer at all. Usually the offer comes in the form of a deposit along with a letter of intent (LOI) that states what the buyer will pay, where the money will come from, the time needed to complete the deal, and a number of other transaction details. Once you accept the LOI, the due diligence (DD) phase begins, where the buyer inspects the business in detail. At the end of DD, the buyer has three options: continue with the deal as defined in the LOI, revoke the offer and get their deposit back, or make a counteroffer to their original LOI. The attorney will start prepping legal documents, the accountant will work with the buyer to verify numbers and start planning the closing transaction, and your financial advisor will consider how all of this will impact your financial future and tax liabilities.

5. Get Paid

The Players: You, your advisors, and the buyer, plus any outside financial source the buyer is using
What Happens: Once DD is approved, the legal documents are finalized and signed by the buyer and seller. If there's bank financing involved, the bank will work with you throughout the closing process, but it generally makes the closing longer. There will be a pre-closing checklist and a proration list where the buyer systematically takes over certain expenses, receives transferred accounts, and more. While closing day is the moment you've been waiting for, in reality it's anti-climactic. You'll sign (or more likely, e-sign) the paperwork, and then the wire transfers will be processed. That day or shortly thereafter, you'll check your bank account and find the

largest deposit you've ever seen! The last remaining items are meeting with your company to announce the sale and introduce the buyer, and then getting started on the transition plan you've put into place.

BUILDING YOUR A-TEAM

If it takes a village to raise a baby, it certainly takes a village to sell a business baby. Unsurprisingly, the people involved in the process of selling your company are going to make or break the deal. You need to make sure you have the best possible team. You'd never work with a general practitioner for a heart valve repair. You'd go straight to a cardiac surgeon, and you should do the same when selling your business. With the exception of attorneys (read the attorney section below for why), you generally get what you pay for. If you want to save a few dollars up front, work with the least expensive provider you can find, and hope for the best results. But if you want to make sure the single most important financial transaction of your life goes smoothly and maximizes the value you receive, shop around until you find the right one, even if they are a little more expensive.

The good news is you don't necessarily need to hire specialists from your particular industry. In my experience, the best advisors are ones who work across all industries. They bring the experience and creativity they learn from other industries and apply it to your deal. They don't get stuck in the "this is the way things work in this industry" attitude. Above all else, the people you hire must have transactional experience with other companies of your size in recent market conditions.

Here's a rundown of the players who will be on your team:

1. **Business Brokers / Investment Bankers**: Brokers and bankers do more than just find you a buyer. In fact, their main responsibility is ensuring a deal gets done with the best possible outcome for you. Even if you find a buyer and get an offer, half of all deals still blow up

during the due diligence phase. Hiring a broker or banker will help reduce this possibility.

- *What's the Difference?* The two main differences between business brokers and investment bankers are the size of the deal and the type of buyer. Business brokers typically handle transactions of businesses with valuations under $25 million, which generally includes companies with revenues up to roughly $40 million. (Again, remember that the average deal size is about $1 million.) Business brokers work with individual buyers, other businesses, and sometimes with private equity (PE) firms. Investment bankers, meanwhile, typically manage transactions of companies with valuations over $25 million. Investment bankers work with PE and large multi-national corporations.
- *What They Handle:* Regardless of whether you're working with a business broker or an investment banker, the sales process is largely the same. After all, brokers and bankers have the same goal—finding the right buyer and getting your business sold. They're responsible for preparing your company to go to market: valuing the company, identifying the most probable buyer, deciding how to market the business, and vetting potential buyers. They help put together the offer, including establishing the purchase price, determining how the buyer should pay, and creating a timeline. Finally, they manage due diligence and the pre-closing and closing activities.
- *Why You Need One:* Lots of people think they can sell their company by themselves, or at least want to try. But you already have one full-time job—running a business. Are you sure you're ready to take on another one simultaneously? Do you have time to market your company and field phone calls from everyone who's ever thought of buying a business? Beyond that, are you qualified to valuate a company, or to vet a potential buyer's ability to pay? Do you

understand how a bank is going to evaluate your company's creditworthiness as they decide whether to fund a loan? The broker is the hub of the wheel, coordinating all the players, anticipating next steps, ensuring deadlines are met, and maintaining positive relationships. A good broker is worth their weight in gold.

- *How They Get Paid:* Brokers and bankers are with the seller from beginning to end, starting with valuation and not ending until the deal is closed. They'll even be there for you during training and transition, although their role is less active by that stage. Ultimately, a good broker will get you more money and a better deal. Most bankers and brokers work on contingency: They get a percentage of the deal, but only get paid if you get paid. Generally, they take a larger percentage for smaller deals, but there's a wide variety of payment structures. Some brokers charge a one-time retainer (it should be small), while most bankers charge a monthly retainer.
- *How to Hire the Right One:* The right broker or banker is mostly a function of one thing: how active they are in the market. They need to have a pulse on what's going on in the business sales market and have strong buyer connections. Success matters, so you should always ask how many deals they've closed in the last year. Thankfully, experience in your industry doesn't matter for most brokers; it's more important that they're involved in the market for companies around your size. Remember that buyers of small companies usually are industry agnostic, so brokers can be, too. (However, bigger buyers, and therefore bankers, usually don't jump across industries.) Ask for referrals from your existing business advisors, and research which brokers have the most businesses for sale in your size range. A broker experienced in dealing with commercial real estate is an added benefit, to help deal with those pesky landlords.

- *What Can Go Wrong:* Beware companies that offer expensive "expert valuations" on your company. If they're not a broker, they don't actually care whether your company gets sold; they just want to collect their fee.

2. **Attorneys**: I get it—people love to hate on lawyers. But when you're selling your business, the only thing worse than having an attorney is *not* having one. Attorneys are the most critical people in the transaction. In some business sales, you can do without other advisors like brokers and accountants—but an attorney is *always* necessary. Your attorney should be well-versed in business sales transactions of companies sized similar to your own.

- *What They Handle:* Obviously, attorneys handle the legal portions of the deal. They take what you agree to with your broker and the buyer, and translate it into legal documents. This can include letters of intent, purchase contracts, promissory notes, and non-compete agreements.
- *Why You Need One:* Even if you forego all other advisors (please don't!), you cannot forego an attorney. You need to protect yourself during and after the transaction. Beyond "papering the deal," they will protect you from liabilities that can arise after the fact. Even though most small business sales go smoothly, there are times when a buyer becomes unhappy with a seller after the purchase. A good attorney will ensure you're not responsible for buyers' remorse or mistakes after you're gone.
- *How They Get Paid:* Most attorneys are paid on an hourly basis, although some use a flat fee instead. Some people worry that attorneys who charge by the hour will milk the time they spend in order to bleed clients dry. For business transaction attorneys, paying by the hour is better—attorneys who charge flat fees often deliver generic, form documents that aren't customized for you.

- *How to Hire the Right One:* Your attorney needs to be one who does business transactions for a living and writes the necessary kinds of documents all the time. A general practitioner or even a general business attorney simply won't do. Ultimately, you'll pay less when you hire a transaction attorney because they have the experience and knowledge to get it done better and faster. And the legal bills you could face to clean up the mess left by the *wrong* attorney could wipe out all the proceeds from your sale, and then some. What makes a good transaction attorney is how familiar they are with transactions of your size and how many deals they do per year. Just about every city has three to four mid-size law firms that specialize in small business mergers and acquisitions, and they should be easy enough to find through your network.
- *What Can Go Wrong:* You don't need to use excessively long documents and the highest-priced attorney from the whitest-shoe firm you can afford. With attorneys and legal issues, bigger isn't always better. An owner of a company with just over $1 million in revenue hired a prestigious law firm to represent her. They usually represented elite PE firms and massive conglomerates, and the draft of the purchase agreement they produced for her was more than 100 pages long. She racked up huge legal fees, and the buyer walked away because the law firm was making the transaction far more complicated than it needed to be. The only winner was the lawyer, who collected a fat fee and moved on.

Additionally, make sure the attorney understands they're not running the show. The broker is the one in charge. Relatedly, it really is important you work with a business transaction attorney. One owner with an excellent business and an enthusiastic buyer decided to use a litigator he knew. Accustomed to a certain way of doing business, the attorney was confrontational and wanted to fight every minor point, even over the objections of the broker. He was probably a great litigator, but he was terrible for a business sale. Several buyers walked away, and the owner wasn't able to sell the company until he engaged a different attorney.

3. Accountants: They're important players in your company before, during, and after your deal.

- *What They Handle:* Before the deal, your accountant will review and verify your financials. During the deal, they maintain the books and keep everything clean and organized. One important role they play is to advise on tax strategies along with your financial advisor (although you may need to engage a small business transactions tax specialist as well). The sale could be taxed on capital gains, as an individual, or in some combination. Your accountant will help determine what's best for you, what you'll pay, and how to make it happen.
- *Why You Need One:* Buyers will hesitate if the owner is managing the books themselves. And even if there is an internal bookkeeper, many buyers want to see an external accountant verifying everything. Even if you're not thinking about selling, it's just good business practice to have a professional managing your financials.
- *How They Get Paid:* For regular maintenance work, you'll continue paying your accountant as you always have. For the additional work they'll take on to prepare for and execute the deal, you can negotiate a flat rate or hourly fee—unlike with attorneys, there's no preference on method.
- *How to Hire the Right One:* Most of the time, the third-party accountant you already use should be fine to use for your deal. After all, they already know the ins and out of your business. There are important exceptions, however. If

you've had a nagging feeling they're not doing a good job, now is the time to switch. And if they haven't done at least one business sale in the last year, better to switch, or at least bring in someone more experienced for the sale, such as a specialized tax advisor.

- *What Could Go Wrong:* Assuming you avoid hacks and crooks, there's no downside here. Hiring an accountant is a no-brainer. It'll save you time, make you more confident in your company financials, and ease the worries of buyers. Your accountant may encourage you to stick with cash accounting for tax purposes, but you should insist on making the change to accrual accounting—it's the gold standard for selling a company. You should do a thorough vetting of your accountant to make sure their clients are happy and have been around for a while. And make sure you don't let the accountant's (likely uninformed) opinions about the value of your business overrule the sage advice of your broker.

4. Financial Advisors: You probably already have a financial advisor, but if you don't, they can be very helpful during your deal, and help set you up for long-term financial security.

- *What They Handle:* Before the deal—and particularly if you're considering retirement within the next ten years—a financial advisor will help you determine what you need out of the sale. They can also help you save money before the sale so your retirement is not entirely dependent on the sale of the company—you must have other avenues for retirement income! This may play a role in what type of buyer you consider and the category and amount of compensation you'll seek. Financial advisors can also help with tax mitigation strategies, especially if you're at least six to twelve months out from sale. After the transaction, they'll help you manage the money you receive and make sure it helps you achieve your goals.

- *Why You Need One:* There are many legally sound strategies and financial vehicles to shield income from tax, defer tax payments, reinvest in your business, and save efficiently for retirement—and I can almost guarantee you don't know most of them.
- *How They Get Paid:* Usually, financial advisors are paid a management fee based on assets under management, generally with little or no upfront fees.
- *How to Hire the Right One:* The best financial advisor is one who works with small business owners and entrepreneurs, and who has the knowledge and resources to structure tax saving strategies. There are lots of investment vehicles business owners can use to save money when they sell. Unfortunately, most financial advisors don't know about them or don't have the resources to execute them.
- *What Could Go Wrong:* Not using a financial advisor experienced in business sales can put at risk all the money you receive from the sale. The owners of a B2B services company walked away with what they thought was a cool $1 million in their pockets on the sale of their business. But their financial advisor wasn't experienced in business transactions, and didn't foresee some grim implications for them. Since the sellers hadn't put in place some simple but critical financial vehicles, they had to pay ordinary income tax on their windfall. Between state and federal taxes, it amounted to nearly 50 percent of what they'd gotten. A more qualified financial advisor could have cut that tax bill in half.

Synergy!

I know, I know, annoying buzzword, but I needed to get your attention after explaining the technical roles your team will fill. Think carefully when selecting your advisors, because they can transform an average deal into a great one. The adage here is true: with the right team, the whole is greater than the sum of its parts. Sometimes starting with one solid player can lead to more. If you find, say, a great business broker, ask them for recommendations of other advisors. They'll know who's excellent at what they do, and they'll help you assemble a stellar squad.

Business owners looking to sell often worry about overpaying their advisors. Unfortunately, I've heard horror stories of, in one case, a firm that charges sellers $50,000 up front for a business valuation, never to be heard from again. Generally, large up-front fees are a bad sign. Business brokers should be paid based on successful completion of the deal or a percentage of the transaction. Retainers for advisors are common, but they should be low; you want your team to be incentivized to get the deal done. Like I said above, you generally get what you pay for, so don't trip over a dollar to pick up a penny.

There's one important caveat to consider for all these advisors: each one needs to stay in their lane. The best teams act like a great rock band on stage: each person has distinct roles and responsibilities, they don't step on each others' toes, and together they collaborate on something spectacular. The ugly truth is that sometimes, other advisors will try to kill your deal, telling you it's a bad idea to sell for any number of reasons. If your broker is telling you that your company is sellable, but your accountant is telling you something different, then your accountant probably has other motives or simply lacks experience. There are situations where your business may not be sellable, but they are few and far between, and your broker would be able to identify them. If your other advisors are working against you, it's time to switch, or at least get a second opinion.

AVOIDING DEAL KILLERS

After all the statistics cited above, you may feel less hopeful about selling your business. There's no need for despair, but you do need to accept reality. Take an honest look at your business baby, warts and all. Now you can take action to make your company as attractive as possible to buyers. One of the most important goals of the preparation process is to mitigate risk. You need to do everything you can to avoid what I call "deal killers"—preventable issues that reduce your buyer pool and make an otherwise-interested buyer walk away from the deal. The strategies below also help you avoid conflicts after the sale. If you're looking to prioritize preparatory steps, this is the place to start. Eliminating these deal killers might not increase the value of your company (although they can), but they will increase the likelihood that your business will be among the elite 20 percent that successfully get a deal.

There are four main categories of risk:

- Financial
- Legal
- Confidentiality
- Regulatory

Financial risks are perhaps the most obvious type of risk. Clearly, most buyers aren't looking for companies that aren't profitable or don't have upside. But sellers need to understand that what buyers consider financial risk might not match their expectations. Even a profitable company with excellent margins can present risks if the accounting books aren't in ship shape or if there's been a history of tax problems. Recall the story above where the company was unsellable until the customer base expanded. If you've been keeping your books by hand, you need to consider moving to computer software. Maybe your company is intertwined with your own personal accounts. All these situations and more can make buyers wary. Chapter 5 explains how to avoid financial risks.

Legal risks are another frequent deal killer. If you have a complex business structure, a history of legal conflicts, or present some other legal challenge to a potential buyer, you risk them walking. If you've been lazy with maintaining minutes of your state-required corporate meetings, if you haven't legally protected important intellectual property, or if your employees don't have non-compete clauses in their contracts, your company will be less attractive. You should also be aware of the potential complications that can result from the actual sales contract itself. While your lawyer may balk, generally the best thing is to keep it simple, stupid. And don't forget about the discussion of landlords and leases earlier in this chapter.

Shhh! Can You Keep a Secret?

Perhaps the least obvious deal killer is confidentiality risk. Some buyers are very concerned about secrecy. Whatever the reason—perhaps they're trying to make a move in the market that will surprise competitors, perhaps they're making a move to please investors, or any other number of things—sellers need to abide by their promises of confidentiality. Clearly, buyers need to do the same. One of the many reasons it's good to have a broker is to ensure the potential buyer isn't just fishing for information—or even something more nefarious, like trying to steal trade secrets. Although this rarely happens, you should ensure your advisors and broker have a tried-and-true system to protect your sale from confidentiality breeches.

Sellers should be concerned about confidentiality, too, even with the most trusted people in their life and business. Selling a business is a long process not for the faint of heart. As much as you may want to involve your team or tell your customers and vendors — don't! Involving these people in the up and down adventure you're about to begin is irresponsible, and even cruel. I've seen a number of sellers ignore this advice, and it always ends the same: employees look for new jobs, customers look for a different provider, and vendors raise their rates. People will forgive you for your secrecy, but you'll never forgive yourself if you ruin your valuation and sale.

Through a mutual friend, a gym owner found a buyer for his company without engaging a broker or taking the business to market. But the mutual friend was also friends with the GM of the gym's biggest competitor. Without intending any harm, the mutual friend mentioned the sale to the rival GM. Unsurprisingly, word quickly got back to the staff at the seller's gym, and over 50 percent of them quit immediately. An average staff person assumes that a business for sale is no better than a business on the brink of collapse. In reality, new owners rarely want to change staff, and instead prefer to keep things running as normally as possible. But because the gym's owner didn't appreciate the need for confidentiality, his business suddenly found itself woefully understaffed and unable to replace them—making the company a risky proposition for any buyer.

Don't Forget about Uncle Sam

In some industries, businesses have a silent partner they may not even know about: the government. Regulatory issues can easily kill deals, and they're harder to resolve than most other challenges facing a sale. Regulatory issues can include:

- **Back Taxes**: Taxes are the only business liabilities that follow the business rather than the owner, and therefore they present a huge risk for buyers. If you are behind on payroll, sales, or other business taxes, it's time to tackle it head on. These need to be cleaned up before the business is listed for sale: either pay them in full or have a negotiated deal in place to pay them at closing. Don't use the employee tax account for emergency cash flow issues. In one extreme example, an owner owed back taxes to the tune of $250,000. The buyer agreed to assume the debt, but it completely wiped out any gain for the sellers.
- **Licensing**: Some industries, such as construction, electrical work, plumbing, and professional services, have licenses that are required by the state or local government. Some can be difficult to transfer, and may have specific additional requirements for a new buyer. Where possible, tie the license to the business instead of to an individual. If that's not possible, try to get an employee licensed rather than the owner.
- **Zoning**: Is your company compliant with local zoning regulations? If not, it could mean the business will need to apply

for rezoning. In the worst case, the business may have to move when a new owner takes over.

MANAGING YOUR EXPECTATIONS

For many owners, the tactical side of selling a company is relatively easy to approach. It involves acknowledging some weaknesses in your business, but mostly it's about developing a plan and then executing it to make the company more attractive to buyers. There are clear goals and measurable results, so it's not totally different from some of what you have probably already been doing as you've run the company.

The emotional side can be much more challenging. If you're like most business owners, a big part of your identity is wrapped up in your business. It's been a huge part of your life, and you've put your whole being into it. It really is like your baby. During the prep-to-sell and sales process, you're going to hear things about your company that you won't want to hear. These are not personal attacks on you. I repeat: do not take it personally! Listen to your broker and advisors when they tell you that a particular change will help you get more value out of the company. Acknowledging failures and making changes is hard, but it's all in the service of your end goal of sipping champagne on the beach.

Don't feel like you're the only one who struggles with managing yourself emotionally throughout this arduous process. It's only natural that you have a strong reaction to something so deeply personal to you, and it happens at some point with every single seller. The key is to have good advisors, someone trustworthy to talk to (like a business coach or a confidential entrepreneur group—not anyone involved in the business!), and an outlet for your stress. The "Resources" section at the end of the book can help point you in the right direction.

Successful sellers know what to expect when selling their business, both tactically and emotionally. And have no illusions—it is emotional. This is your baby, after all. Owners need to understand how to prepare themselves for the "after." Your day-to-day is going to be very different, financially and personally, after you sell. Just like you have a plan for selling your company, you need to have a plan to deal with all the changes in your life. This will require some honest self-reflection, and the more realistic you can be, the better.

If you don't have a plan for the future, there will be times in the deal process when you find yourself fighting over a meaningless item or dragging your heels for seemingly no reason. You may not realize it at the time, but there's a good chance you'll be doing it because you fear the future. It's important that you're running *towards* something new, rather than *away* from your business. The more you can give yourself something to look forward to after the sale, the better you will be able to handle the emotional swings of the deal process.

Owners also need to check their egos throughout the sales process. Ego can appear in a variety of subtle ways, but it most often rears its ugly head around company valuation and how you're going to be paid for it. Despite how much you love your company and how successful you consider it, the valuation probably won't be as high as you think it should be. Remember that valuation is a mathematical formula that comes down to assets and profits. Buyers aren't going to pay for the passion you've put into the company, and banks won't finance your social media savvy.

Unrealistic sales price expectations can blind owners to a good deal. The owner of a craft workshop wanted to sell her company. It was a great business: large, profitable, and well-run with established staff. She had created prestige around the company by engaging with very popular national artisans, and the profitability reflected it. She received a number of solid offers around $3 million with beneficial terms, in line with the valuation calculated by her broker. Unfortunately, the owner refused to sell for less than $7 million. She simply couldn't understand why buyers weren't willing to pay for the reputation she'd so carefully built. Eventually she received over a dozen similar offers, but she refused each one, and the business never sold.

In another case, a retail store owner used some creative marketing to build an impressive social media following. His business spiked over 800 percent with the new campaign, and although revenue returned to the status quo the next year, he maintained and even kept growing the large social media following. Shortly thereafter, he decided to sell the business. He wanted to ask for a price based on the revenue from his peak year. After all, the company's social media accounts gave them access to a huge pool of customers. Buyers disagreed; they weren't willing to pay more for a social media channel that was no longer converting followers into customers. It also made the buyers wonder whether there was an issue with the product that prevented customers from becoming repeat buyers.

The negotiation process is another time when seller egos can get bruised. Buyers can unintentionally offend sellers during meetings. They may ask why you attempted a particular growth strategy, or why you never explored a certain customer base. Maybe you have and maybe you haven't—either way, the result the buyers were looking for wasn't achieved. Buyers who do this aren't necessarily being critical. They're just trying to identify potential growth areas. You want them to be excited about this search—it's what will inspire them to close the deal! They know you're the expert, and they want your knowledge. Instead of getting defensive—and possibly giving a negative impression of your business—share what you know, and be ready to acknowledge that even if you tried a particular strategy and failed, they may be much better positioned to execute it well. You're trying to walk away from the company because you want to move on, but they're asking questions because they're enthusiastic about possibly running the company. You must keep a positive energy around the discussions.

I spoke about the importance of feeling that you're running towards something new, rather than away from your business. For this reason, it's usually best to make a clean exit from the company. Staying on after the sale rarely works. You've been your own boss for a long time, and it can be incredibly uncomfortable working for someone else in the company you personally nurtured for years. Some owners experience depression or a sense of loss after they sell their business. When I sold my wine company, I went from working seventy hours a week to . . . nothing. I felt like I'd lost my identity. I never imagined I'd mourn the loss of a business I didn't want to be involved in anymore, but that's exactly what happened. Whether you're starting another company, focusing on your health, getting more involved in charitable causes, or devoting yourself fully to golf, you need to have a plan for how to occupy your time. You can also consider counseling to help you manage the adjustment.

KEY TAKEAWAYS:

- Preparing and selling your company can take up to 24 months, or even longer. The more prep work you do before you even consider selling, the better the chances your company sells, and at a higher price.
- Hiring a great sales advisory team can be the difference between selling and languishing on the market forever.
- A business sale has five steps: Prepare for the Sale, Go to Market, Find and Qualify a Buyer, Negotiate a Deal, and Get Paid. Own the process by understanding the rules for each step.
- Selling your company is not just a business transaction—it's a major life change. Don't underestimate the emotion that will emerge.

TO DO NOW:

- Eliminate any deal killers you've identified in your business. Engage with outside experts wherever necessary.
- Take a realistic view of your future. How much longer can you run your business? How much longer do you *want* to? Establish your timeline from there.

CHAPTER 3

People

As any good business owner will tell you, people are the heart of your business. Your employees, your customers, and your vendors are possibly your most valuable assets. This cast of characters can be one of the biggest selling points of your business—or one of the biggest sticking points. Sellers must understand how people can drive the value of their company; they particularly must understand how their own role can make all the difference in closing the deal.

These key stakeholders will impact the value of your business. Understandably, it all starts at the top.

THE OWNER

This chapter is all about the people who make your business possible, and you'll notice there's one person conspicuously absent from the discussion about the value of your company: you. One of the most important parts of preparing to sell your company is transitioning your role from *operator* to *owner*. An operator works *in* the business running the day-to-day, while an owner works *on* the business strategizing about growth and long-term vision. Whether it's the daily grind, managing personnel, pursuing new customers, production, or other traditional entrepreneurial roles, your job is to put others in charge, creating a well-oiled machine that doesn't need you. It is exponentially more difficult to sell a business whose owner is the operator.

It's critical you make this transition so you get a better price. Buyers want to ensure that the company retains all the institutional knowledge it needs to continue successfully, and that they won't have to hire someone to replace you (which would reduce the SDE, or seller's discretionary earnings, of the company; see Chapter 1 for more on SDE, and Chapter 5 for more on finances generally). You should not be an irreplaceable element of your business; buyers will be less interested in paying top dollar for a company with a cult of personality built around a charismatic owner. Removing yourself can increase the multiple you receive by 0.5x to 2x! It also makes your company more attractive to those outside your industry, which increases your buyer pool. At the very least, you should be able to go away on vacation for a few weeks and not have the business implode without you.

Not removing yourself from the business—and particularly from critical functions—can decrease the value you receive on closing and can limit your ability to walk away cleanly. Above all, buyers fear that when the deal closes, customers and employees will leave. As a result, you should remove yourself first from the roles that impact these risks:

1. **Revenue-Generating Roles**: Whatever role in your business that is most critical to revenue is the one that needs to be the least reliant on you. Consider what role you play in sales and marketing. What happens when you go away? What process can you put in place to make up that difference? This is a good exercise to undertake not only in preparing to sell, but also in managing your businesses normally. Understandably, an owner is crucial to generating revenue in a new business. At some point, however, that dynamic needs to flip. A useful key performance metric is the percentage of revenue generated by the owner. Over time, it should decline to less than 30 percent.

2. **Customer-Facing Roles**: These roles are typically customer service, account management, or some roles related to production. Customers should feel they're doing business with the company, not with you. In fact, it's a good thing when customers don't know who the owner is. Preparation here is important, because losing customers after the sale can impact your takeaway from the deal. If you have an earnout, you could miss milestones if you bleed too much revenue as a result of customer defection. Similarly, if the sales contract calls for you to assist in the transition process, and you lose too many customers, you could face a legal challenge from the buyer for failing to meet the terms of the agreement.
3. **Production Roles**: If you produce a physical product or a proprietary service, you should remove yourself from this role, which may require you to train someone on your staff. The likelihood of finding a buyer who can replicate your skills is very low.
4. **Employee Management Roles**: This is usually the last seat the owner leaves. It's not critical, but if it moves the business into a true absentee-ownership business, it can make a significant difference. It can increase your sale price and significantly widen your buyer pool. It may also generate interest from strategic and investment buyers, who pay more than the individual buyers.

The owner's role in producing goods should not be overlooked. The owner of a company that designed and built bespoke medical prosthetics wanted to retire. He had a strong, experienced staff that took good care of almost every single element of the business. The owner, however, never trained anyone in one fundamental task: some of the prosthetics required actual carving by hand, and the owner was the only one who knew how to do it. It was a great company, but no buyer would touch it unless the owner agreed to stay on and train a cadre of staff how to do the carving. Ultimately, the owner had to agree to a lower purchase price and stay on for a full year, working for the new owner until the new carvers were adequately trained—which ended up taking only six months. If the seller had the foresight to train someone before he sold, think of the sale price he could have gotten!

Moving from an operator to an owner can be another emotional struggle for a seller. It requires letting go of control of everything in the business, including the things you still like or are particularly good at. You must push through this wall, because it's one of the single most impactful things you can do to increase the sale price of your company.

YOUR EMPLOYEES

Having strong management and experienced staff in your company will immediately make it more attractive to potential buyers. Buyers love established teams, especially when they are adept at running the company without much involvement from the owner. As discussed above, part of your preparations for sale will be to remove yourself as much as possible from the day-to-day running of the business. As a result, employee tenure is a critical factor buyers consider.

Have your employees create manuals on their jobs, documenting their responsibilities and processes. Use the opportunity to refine job descriptions, improve onboarding and training, and create more efficient collaboration. The more documentation you have on internal functions, the more confident a buyer will feel about running the company without you.

Secrets, Secrets Are No Fun . . . but Revealing Them Can Blow Up Your Deal

Many owners ask whether they should tell their employees they're thinking about selling. Some owners feel they "owe" it to their employees to be honest, or feel it's "disloyal" to keep them in the dark. This is well intentioned—and terribly dangerous. Employees are not entrepreneurs; they're not used to experiencing the ups and downs of running a company. Most employees are terrified if they hear the owner is selling. They fear that they could be squeezed out during the transition, that their position won't be secure in the new structure, that the new owners won't appreciate their value, or that the new entity will lose the culture and personality that made your company a pleasant place to work. As a result, they may feel the need to bolt after the sale—or worse, bolt before the sale is finalized, which could put the deal at risk.

One owner confided in a long-time employee about a pending sale. The employee, understanding that retaining him would be a key element to the sale, blackmailed the seller for $15,000 to remain with the company. Also recall the story in Chapter 2 about the gym that lost half of its employees overnight when they found out the business was for sale. When word gets out that a company is for sale, employees, customers, and vendors assume the worst and exit en masse. Pretty soon, you won't have a business left to sell. Such a dramatic ending is rare, but it's a controllable risk you must mitigate.

When employees find out about a sale *after* the deal is done, they're usually quite accepting. What they want is to be assured they'll be paid the same or more, and almost all buyers are happy to comply. Buyers work to make the employees' lives better than before. A key element to the transition plan should be to create great messaging when you inform the employees. Your input on this will help the buyer feel more confident in their ability to retain employees.

In reality, most buyers really want employees to stay, and work hard to limit any disruption to business as usual. They understand they need employees who know how to run the business, not only to get through the day-to-day, but also to grow in the future. Most buyers actually offer new benefits to employees to demonstrate their commitment to the existing team. Buyers don't want to worry about their newly-purchased company falling apart as soon as the sale goes through. They want the company to continue functioning at least as efficiently and maintain its forward progress on growth. If you've done the work of stepping back from an operator role into an owner role, your employees will already feel more empowered to function without you, and the buyers will be even less likely to mess with a well-functioning system.

Buyers Obsess Over Employees

Many buyers are concerned about generating loyalty from the staff. When the buyer of a pet store was introduced to his new staff, he told them how excited he was to work with them and immediately announced his intention to offer healthcare to all of them, a benefit they hadn't had under the previous owner. Ten years later, the buyer still owns the company, and has had very little staff turnover. Now, you may be surprised the buyer went right to health insurance as opposed to some other benefit part-time employees often lack, such as paid time off. Upon evaluating all the options, the buyer decided health care would make the biggest emotional connection with the employees. After considering the high cost of turnover endemic to the industry, health care also wasn't that much more expensive than other benefit options.

Owners can help reduce buyer concerns by instituting incentives, such as bonuses or equity opportunities, to encourage employee retention. The owner of an interior design company hired a general manager to run the business. The employee's contract included a five-year retention bonus, which the owner and GM had renewed several times over the years. With the GM successfully running the company and incentivized to stay, the owner was able to remove herself from the business. When the owner went to sell the company, she was able to attract buyers from a variety of industries, since they wouldn't need to worry about running the business. Wisely, the owner also made sure the retention bonus contract was assignable to the next owner. She received top dollar for her company and was able to make a clean break.

By contrast, the owner of an IT company hired a GM to run the business, but didn't include any sort of retention incentive. The GM was running the company efficiently, and like the interior design business, the owner was able to step away. Unfortunately, just as the owner took the company to market, the GM decided to move on to another opportunity. There was no bad intent, as the GM didn't know about the sale, but it forced the owner to take the company off the market and once again run the business himself. For two years, he tried to find another GM, but eventually decided to sell the company anyway, for less money, because it was too difficult. By not providing the GM a reason to stay, the owner lost two years and a good deal of sale value. Owners need to provide more than just emotional reasons for key employees like managers to stay with a company. A strong relationship and a store of goodwill aren't enough, so owners should create financial or legal incentives as well.

Owners who are preparing to sell also should consider the legal relationships they have with their employees. Many staff members like to be full-time employees and enjoy the benefits that come with that status. Others, however, are open to different types of relationships, such as independent contractors and freelancers. These employment structures generally place less burden on the company, making it more attractive to buyers, and can reduce the legal complications of the sale. You should ensure these contract agreements are assignable to a new owner so they don't have to renegotiate the relationships and pay structures.

You also need to be open and honest with the buyer about any promises you've made to employees regarding equity, promotions, and other benefits. Chances are the buyer will be eager to keep the promises in order to retain the employees, but they'll need to account for these realities when they make their offer. Once you're negotiating with a buyer, don't give employees a pay raise or any non-routine bonuses without first discussing it with the buyer. In fact, don't give any unscheduled raises once you've taken the company to market.

Paying more to your employees reduces the SDE, which decreases the value of the company.

As you're preparing your company for sale, be very thoughtful about hiring new employees. On one hand, adding another employee impacts your SDE, which will reduce the value you receive on the sale. On the other hand, a new team member who shores up a weak area, opens a new avenue of business, or brings along an impressive clientele could be a wonderful asset that would improve SDE. This is also a good opportunity to explore the other employment relationships mentioned above (with existing employees, bring it up during your regular contract renegotiation so it seems all in the course of regular business).

Keep in mind that the solution to replacing yourself in certain roles is not limited to hiring a new full-time employee. Alternatively, you could:

- Assign the task to an existing employee.
- Automate the task with technology.
- Delegate the task to a new employee (part- or full-time) or freelancer, or outsource it to an outside firm.
- Eliminate the task if it's no longer necessary or efficient.

Whatever you do, remember that a new hire should produce exponential results for both your top and bottom lines, or should help you take a significant step back from the business. Additionally, consider cross-training employees so no one person is irreplaceable. You could even consider outsourcing some of your internal functions. One client hired an outside accounting firm to replace his internal accounting team. In addition to reducing risk from the buyer's perspective, it also saved him $150,000 per year. This greatly increased the SDE, and translated directly into more cash in his pocket at closing.

YOUR CUSTOMERS

You can't make money without customers, and buyers won't be interested in a company without plenty of them. Customers play the single most important role in determining business value. If you have a client concentration issue—where one client accounts for a huge chunk of your business—your company is a big risk for buyers. In my experience, companies that receive the highest multiples have a top client that accounts for no more than 30 percent of total revenue.

There are other areas where over-concentration can negatively impact company value. You need to ask yourself three questions about your customers:

- **Does one middleman or referral partner generate the bulk of your business?**
  Examples could include: one general contractor, one CPA firm, one developer, the state, or the city government. Generally, you should expand to more referral partners. If you have (or need to maintain) an exclusive arrangement with the existing partner, explore a new specialty vertical that would allow you to create relationships with entities that don't compete with your current partner.
- **Does one type of customer or industry provide a large percentage of your business?**
  If so, what happens if that industry takes a turn for the worse? In Texas, many companies specialize in working with the oil and gas industry. It's big business, but highly susceptible to fluctuations in the price of oil, which often causes layoffs and reduced budgets in that sector. Every type of company that services the industry, from recruiting to IT, is impacted when this happens. Other industries highly susceptible to economic trends are real estate, construction, luxury goods, and travel. If you're too concentrated in one industry, brainstorm other

industries that could use your products or services with minimal adjustments on your part.

- **Do most of your customers come from the same marketing source?**
  Every company needs a variety of marketing sources. Marketing strategies and their efficacy change so fast that only a diversified marketing plan can protect a company from the roller coaster ride of new business inflow. One client generated all their leads from the online advertising. When their account was suspended by a search provider (over a false claim!), all their leads disappeared overnight. Thankfully they quickly deployed other strategies to generate business while they straightened things out online, but had they not been able to pivot so quickly, it would have resulted in zero new business for the month. You don't want to find yourself in a similar situation.

Customer concentration issues can take some time to solve. A sign production company owner won a large contract with the local branches of a big box store. The relationship accounted for approximately 85 percent of the company's revenue. The owner knew he wanted to sell eventually, but he was savvy. He recognized his client structure wasn't just going to reduce his ability to sell; it was also a risk to the long-term viability of the company even if he didn't sell. He started small, assigning one existing sales representative to focus on generating deals with small companies. The deals were often only for a few hundred dollars, but they were plentiful and actually produced higher margins than the big box contract. After three years, the small business sales team had grown exponentially, and they accounted for more revenue than the big box relationship. The company became larger and more profitable, and sold for full asking price. Without the lead time the owner was able to devote to this effort, he would not have gotten full value for his company.

Additionally, before you put your company up for sale, you need to have a strong sales team in place that functions independently from you. The company's ability to draw in and maintain clients cannot be dependent on your influence or charisma. Buyers want to see clients who have strong relationships with the company as a whole, not just with the owner. Buyers also want a sales team with a strong track record of performance and a robust pipeline of potential new customers. Further, buyers like to see a clear future in a company's relationships with existing customers. If a company has long-term contracts in place with clients, particularly contracts that allow for assignment of the contract to a successor company or new owner, buyers will consider the company that much more valuable.

YOUR VENDORS

In many ways, the relationships potential buyers want to see with existing customers are the same they want to see with existing vendors. Of course, it requires time to develop these deep relationships with vendors, so if you haven't established them already, you need to begin as soon as possible. And here, too, you want the relationship to be with the company, and not with you, the owner. This means the handshake deal you've had for years with a vendor will not cut it. You need to make sure the buyer will enjoy the same price and terms as you, otherwise the company's sale price will decrease. If it's not in writing, it may as well not exist.

As with customers, potential buyers want to see varied rather than concentrated vendors. Supply chain security is critical to your company's ability to function and generate revenue. Customers get nothing—and the company doesn't get paid—when you can't access the raw materials you need. Buyers don't want to risk failing to deliver to a client because one important vendor is experiencing an issue. Your company should have multiple vendors for every resource required. If there are few suppliers, or even only one, you should have contracts with them that guarantee your company will get preferential delivery should there be any issues. And as always, these contracts should be assignable.

Also as with customers, sellers should aim to have assignable vendor contracts that will remain in effect should the seller's (or vendor's!) company get acquired. These contracts also should lock in the prices and benefits guaranteed to your company, and should establish that the new company will be able to negotiate the next contract with the same status the existing company would be granted. The sooner you can start making the necessary changes to your vendor relationships, the better. As with existing employees and customers, aim to adjust these relationships during regular contract renegotiations.

To understand your current scenario, you need to examine your vendor contracts as soon as possible—preferably before you even sign them. A successful niche beverage distribution company was for sale, and the owner thought he would be able to secure a great price because he was the exclusive distributor to the whole state for a popular national beverage manufacturer. He didn't realize, however, the incredible power the manufacturer had over his company. Nearly at the end of due diligence, the owner discovered that his exclusive contract wasn't assignable to anyone else, *and* that the manufacturer would have to approve any sale of the distribution company. This gave the manufacturer tremendous power over the future of the company, and a more nefarious actor could have killed not only this deal, but also the owner's ability to sell altogether. Thankfully, the manufacturer was easy to work with, and the deal did go through, although it was delayed eight weeks. There's no doubt other powerful manufacturers wouldn't have been as accommodating.

Having multiple vendors and planning ahead can make a significant difference when you go to sell. For example, in certain food retail businesses, your suppliers play an outsized role in determining your margins, and thus profitability. A coffee shop owner who was preparing to sell started engaging multiple vendors, and was able to create competition among the vendors to secure his business for the long term. A bakery owner, however, only had one supplier for an important ingredient, and when the supplier found out she was selling, he took the opportunity to raise prices. The baker didn't have time to pursue any other vendors before closing the deal, and her sale price suffered as a result.

YOUR PARTNERS

Finally, owners need to get buy-in on the sale from their partners and investors. The legal structure of partnerships and investments can create many limitations for a potential seller, so business owners should approach these relationships with caution—and a lawyer!

Whether dealing with a partner or investor, an owner should understand exactly what their obligations are to the other party. If it's a partnership, how do decisions get made? In an equal partnership, what happens in the case of disagreements? How will the proceeds and any remaining assets be divided? If it's a silent partner or investor, does the owner have to do anything more than notify them of a sale? Does the investor have voting rights? Does the owner have to secure the investor's approval of a sale? Does the investor have the right to be involved in negotiations? All of these terms should be specified in the investor agreement, which the owner must understand fully before beginning the sales process. Otherwise an investor could kill a deal at the eleventh hour.

Save the Drama for Your Mama

Family businesses can be wonderful, but they can also tear families apart. A family owned a hugely successful distribution company the mother had founded and built from scratch. Her dream was to leave the company in the hands of her son and daughter, who would keep the company in the family and leave to it their children as well. Unfortunately, after the mother's untimely death, nothing went according to her wishes. The son and daughter simply could not get along. After fighting for years over which of them would run the company, the siblings lawyered up and sued each other. The court-ordered mediator asked my firm to help sort things out.

While there were some genuine business issues in dispute, the problems at their core were personal and emotional. The son wanted out of the business, believing it was time to move on and end the family turmoil. The daughter believed that by selling, they were abandoning their mother's legacy. Throughout the internal struggle, the company somehow continued to perform incredibly well. I was left to wonder just how well it could have done without the infighting. Truly, the siblings wasted something special.

While an extreme example, this situation reflects the unfortunate reality that partnerships, and particularly family partnerships, can come to fiery conclusions. Friendships are torn apart, families are destroyed, and often the businesses crumble under the pressure. More often than not, the problems are far more personal than they are business-related. Selling a company is more than just a financial transaction; it is a highly emotional decision marking the end of something deeply personal. It's all the more emotional when you're dealing with people you care (or cared) about.

Partnerships are often entered into with enthusiasm and optimism. Unfortunately, sometimes one partner does all the work, while the other reaps the benefits, or there are disagreements over strategy, compensation, and moving on from the company. You should set up the business with the understanding that eventually it will come to an end. Include an exit agreement as part of the initial contract, and determine now how decisions will be made then. Be particularly careful in fifty-fifty partnerships with equal rights. As they say, the difference between 51 percent and 49 percent is everything. If problems do arise, it's a good idea to bring in professional business advisors to help partners work through them before they become irreparable.

KEY TAKEAWAYS:

- Transitioning your role from operator to owner can immediately increase the multiple your company receives by 0.5x to 2x.
- When deciding to add employees or other help, determine what impact it will have on profitability. Don't risk SDE without an outsized reward in profit.
- If you have partners or investors, understand any exit limitations. If there are no exit guidelines, create clear ones. Engage a professional to facilitate the conversation.

TO DO NOW:

- List all the roles you fill in your company, and decide how to eliminate those responsibilities over time. Go to exitfactor.com/maximizebusiness for an Owner Responsibility Worksheet.
- Analyze your customer makeup to determine whether you have a concentration issue. If you do, work to eliminate it.
- Review all customer, vendor, and employment agreements (including 1099 contractors) to ensure they are assignable to a new owner. If they're not, make this change at the next regular contract renegotiation.

CHAPTER 4

Market

You may imagine your business baby is so beautiful that no one will be able to resist its charms. Unfortunately, it's just that: your imagination. Most buyers assume, until proven otherwise, that all business babies were beat with an ugly stick. Your job is to prove them wrong. You want your business to sparkle on the market. The better the appearance, the more buyers will be interested, which can drive competition and ultimately sale price.

In some respects, marketing a business for sale is different from traditional marketing. Your broker, for example, is unlikely to take out an ad on TV announcing to the world you're selling your business. Instead, they'll probably use specialized, private networks and confidential strategies. But in other ways, sales is sales: you want your product (your company) to be as attractive to as many people as possible so you get the most value for it.

VALUE PROPOSITION

A good salesperson knows that no matter the product, you need a clear and compelling value proposition. Kevin Daum explains it best in his book *ROAR: Getting Heard in the Sales and Marketing Jungle*—a value proposition is the ability to identify the customer's pain, clearly state the objective solution, and communicate your company's specific differentiation, which is what your company can do that your competitors cannot without great effort or expense.

You'll need this same kind of value proposition when selling your business. This will require you to do an honest evaluation of your company and get to the bottom of what makes your company valuable and ready for growth. Four main elements will drive your value proposition to buyers:

- Business Reputation
- Customers
- Products and Services
- Opportunities

Begin with Basics!

Now, these four are the single most important elements, but don't forget to use your common sense. Before you have an open house when you're trying to sell your home, you spiff it up. You do a deep clean, tidy your things, and maybe have a stager come in so you can make the house look as good as possible. There's no need to use a stager in your offices, but some basic cleanup is highly advisable. Spend some time cleaning and tidying your physical (and virtual!) space:

- Organize your office and make sure it's cleaned regularly while it's on the market. Buyers will be touring!
- If you have inventory, do a cleanse or even a mass sale to clear out bad or outdated items, or those that have sat on the shelf for too long.
- Examine your physical and virtual documents and reduce the clutter. If something isn't necessary anymore, get rid of it. It'll be one less thing for the buyer to inspect.
- Clean your databases so you can show an organized accounting of your customers and prospects. Run deduplication processes so you are not overestimating the number of accounts or potential revenue.

These things are basic and easily overlooked or postponed, but they matter. One of my brokers was selling an excellent industrial manufacturing company. It was highly profitable and generating a ton of interest from buyers. The process was moving so fast that the broker and seller hadn't had time to walk through the business property together. Still, when an anxious buyer wanted a warehouse tour, they decided to allow it. When the broker arrived with the buyer, the place was a mess. There was stuff all over the yard: old equipment, boxes, workbenches, and more. Inside, there were piles of papers, leftovers from a luncheon, and tools scattered about. But the most embarrassing part was right next to the front door: an old, dusty, cracked toilet. It was clear from the remaining manufacturer's stickers that the toilet had never been used and was just being moved to the trash, but the broker was understandably mortified. The broker could see the question on the buyer's face: if the business was so physically messy, was it equally messy financially or logistically? Thankfully, the buyer had a good sense of humor about the incident, but the optics could have caused major problems.

YOU SHOULD GIVE A DAMN ABOUT YOUR REPUTATION

Obviously, buyers want companies with strong brand recognition and impeccable reputations. Buyers evaluate reputation by asking the following questions:

- Does the company have a recognizable brand in its industry and market?
- Does the company have a good reputation for its products or services, customer service, and business practices?
- Is the company using up-to-date, effective marketing tools and technologies?
- Can the brand stand on its own without the current owner?

Potential buyers will also examine the length of time your company has been in business (the longer, the better!), whether the company has created partnerships in the industry and strong links within the community, and the strength of your online presence.

There are several actions you can take to improve your performance in these areas, although some take more time than others. Brand recognition can be improved with strategies such as public relations campaigns and industry awards. Networking and referral agreements can deepen relationships within your industry and in the community. You can improve your online presence, and possibly your company's reputation, by expanding your social media outreach and closely monitoring your company's online reviews.

Make sure your company's marketing strategy for clients is strong and industry-appropriate. This assumes, of course, that you actually have a cohesive, comprehensive marketing plan. A stunning number of small businesses don't, and it's one of the most significant hurdles owners face when trying to sell their company. Depending on the industry, the average company spends 1 percent to 15 percent of their gross revenue per year on marketing. If your spend is lower than the industry average for companies of your size, you might want to consider increasing it. To make it cost-neutral, shave expenses in other areas that do not directly impact sales. Remember, you don't need to design a marketing program on your own; there are lots of experts available to support you.

A Virtual Debacle

Whether it's from Google, Yelp, a customer's social media, etc., some owners get sweaty even thinking about online reviews of their company. They prefer to keep their heads in the sand rather than face what could be a trove of bad news. Avoidance, however, is not a strategy, particularly if you're trying to sell the business. Most potential buyers will mystery shop your business, which will include a deep dive into the online profile of the company (and the owner . . . more on that shortly). They'll be highly focused on online reviews and how the seller has handled them. We've already discussed that buyers won't pay for social media savvy—but they will hightail it away from companies with multiple bad online reviews. Reviews are also an important part of Google's algorithms, so it's in your best interest to clean them up even if you're not planning to sell.

No doubt you've heard plenty of horror stories about crazy customers wreaking havoc in online reviews. The owner of a handyman business rang the doorbell at his next appointment and was greeted by a frantic, wild-eyed, barely-clothed woman. Upon entering the house, the business owner immediately noticed drug paraphernalia, and it became obvious the woman was high on something other than life. Wisely, he explained to the woman that he would be unable to help her that day, and left. A few days later, the owner noticed a harshly critical review online in which the woman accused him of failing to help her and then leaving without explanation. He responded to the post and explained, in full, glorious detail, what had occurred. They got into a mean-spirited back-and-forth that lasted nearly a month and was in full view of the public. Once things go online, they're hard to erase. When the owner tried to sell his business two years later, the buyer found the argument. It nearly killed the deal, and although the buyer was able to make it work, the owner had to accept a lower price.

Sometimes bad reviews come from nefarious actors with a close relationship with the company. A finance company had to fire an employee for cause, and he was highly agitated about it. To get back at the company, he created fifteen different accounts and wrote a bunch of bad reviews. Thankfully, the owner discovered the problem quickly and reported them to Google as fake reviews. Before they were removed by Google, she also responded to them publicly and clarified that they were from a disgruntled former employee. Her quick actions saved her a great deal of headache a few years later when she decided to sell the firm.

On the other end of the spectrum, a strong reputation and great online reviews can transform an unsellable company into a highly sought one. The owner of a B2B services company was highly involved in the business and had few team members who would remain after the sale. It seemed to the owner it would be extremely challenging to sell. The company, however, had been around for over a decade and had an impeccable reputation, not only in the business community but also online. The company had hundreds of four- and five-star reviews, which helped them stay at the top of search results and resulted in a steady flow of business without spending on marketing. As soon as the company was listed, an out-of-state strategic buyer immediately jumped on the opportunity. Based on the reputation and customer flow, they offered $1 million for the company, with a quick close and 90 percent cash to the seller at closing. Not bad for an owner who thought the company would be worthless!

People who write online reviews tend to come from the extremes of customer interactions: most had either a really great or really terrible experience. There are three key strategies to managing online reviews:

- **Respond publicly to all reviews**: It may be uncomfortable, but this is most important with negative reviews. There's no need to be like the handyman owner and go back and forth with them in a public forum; simply express that you understand there was a problem and that you'll be reaching out privately. And don't ignore the good reviewers! Thank them for being a client and express your enthusiasm for continuing to work with them.
- **Reach out privately to negative reviewers**: When you discover a dissatisfied customer online, get in touch with them as soon as possible. Responding in a thoughtful, service-oriented, non-defensive manner can convert a former customer into a recurring one. Plus, reviewers often change their tunes: in a full two-thirds (really!) of cases, the user either takes down the negative review or goes back to change it into a positive one.

- **Assemble more positive reviews to outweigh negative ones**: Hopefully you have plenty of satisfied clients, so use them! People are usually happy to share their good experiences, even without incentive. You can consider using a specialized agency to improve your online reviews, but proceed with caution: Google knows some less ethical agencies use paid reviewers to pad stats, and Google will penalize your search performance in response.

Any time you're dealing with negative reviews, remember you don't have to prove you're right; you just have to get what you want—which is a good reputation for your company. Don't take on the reviewer point by point, defending your actions and criticizing their motives. React calmly and politely, publicly acknowledge the concern, and take care of the details privately. The only time you should really defend yourself is when you have a troll, like the former employee above. And even then, your defense is reporting the fake review, not taking on the reviewer.

There Are No Company Secrets

Finally, understand that buyers will investigate *you* online, too. Before you hire a new employee, you probably Google their name and check out their Facebook and Instagram accounts. Buyers do the same thing for sellers. If your accounts aren't private, seriously consider using that feature. If they're public, take a deep dive into your past posts. Remove anything remotely political or controversial. Even if you believe them strongly, it's not worth the risk of driving away potential buyers. You can consider asking your employees to keep their accounts private as well, and to refrain from political or controversial opining on public forums.

You may also need to remove posts that seem innocuous. Consider everything from the potential buyer's point of view. If you regularly post about your recurring case of The Mondays, the buyer is going to feel like running the company is a major drag. That post about your frustration with your employees isn't going to inspire the buyer's confidence in your staff. One seller had a long history of sharing personal details about her life online. It was an authentic, intimate examination of her struggles and triumphs, and in any other situation, it might have been admirable. Unfortunately, the buyer felt they made the seller look somewhat unstable. The buyer wasn't comfortable entering into such an important transaction with the seller, and she rescinded her offer for the company. It may seem unfair, but considering that buying a company is one of the most expensive decisions a buyer will ever make, it's not unreasonable. When posting anything online, act like everybody's watching.

Prepare to Just Walk Away, Renee

Another important element of business reputation is transitioning your company into an entity entirely separate from you, the owner. All brand development strategies discussed here will simultaneously establish your company independently from you. There are some explicit additional steps that may be necessary. If the "About Us" section of your company website is all about your journey through entrepreneurship and your passion for the business, buyers will notice. If you're an integral part of your marketing materials, such as functioning as the pitch man in TV spots, appearing in the newsletter, or clients quoting your personal touch in testimonials, your company won't appear to stand on its own. Further, if you named the company after yourself, most situations will call for a new business name.

The owner of a successful skiing equipment store in a vacation hotspot wanted to sell his company. It was a very desirable business: it had a perfect location, had been around for years, was popular with locals and tourists, and was quite profitable. The owner had also retained the same seasonal employees for years on end, a luxurious rarity in seasonal retail, and didn't have many day-to-day responsibilities. The owner, however, was closely associated with the brand. He'd named the store after himself, and the store's walls and website were full of pictures of him and his family. He'd also created a popular line of clothing he named after his kids, and used them as models. Unfortunately, he ignored his broker's advice to disassociate himself from the brand, and he's never been able to sell, despite the strong financials.

CUSTOMER BASE

As we discussed in Chapter 3, the diversity of your customer base is critical to how a buyer will evaluate your business. You need to make sure that your customers find you via a variety of sources (such as middlemen, referral partners, and marketing sources) and that they include a number of different industries. Having a good mix of customers means your company will not suffer disproportionately when one referral source or industry dries up. It also means the company will have room to grow its client base into a number of different segments, which will make buyers smile. Be sure to check out Chapter 3 to get all the details.

PRODUCTS AND SERVICES

Just as with your customer base, diversity of products is also critical to how buyers will view your company. Buyers want to see multiple ways they will be able to make money in your business. This means developing, or at least setting up the basic infrastructure for, new and different products and services. See how you can naturally expand your offerings to clients, perhaps with a deeper or wider array of what you already do. Design smaller options for smaller clients, too, as a way to increase your customer base. If you're a product-based company, consider adding services, and vice versa.

Get Stuck on Repeat

Buyers want to see that the customer base is strong and repeatable. Over and over, buyers ask, "What kind of recurring revenue does the company have?" Recurring revenue is predictable income that can be counted on in the future. It is important to buyers because it stabilizes a business and reduces their risk in the future. The most obvious form of recurring income is a subscription-based business model. You may immediately think of Netflix or a home security business, but you don't have to be a tech company to make this feasible: if there's a repeated need for your product or service, it can be made into recurring income. You could also consider selling a platform product or service with the opportunity for upsells. Other models to explore include memberships, associations, certifications, buyers' clubs, or even licensing your product or service to a third party. Take a look at all of your sources of revenue and get creative! How can you turn a one-time order into a recurring one? Even my business brokerage firm has recurring revenue!

There are also other ways of achieving the same, recurring end. See if you can turn one-time contracts into multiyear or automatically renewing deals (making sure they're assignable to a new owner). Janitorial service companies often find it very simple to change their monthly contracts into automatically renewing annual contracts. A fire services company examined their business and discovered they already had recurring income; they just hadn't defined it as such. Every six months, they inspected their clients' fire extinguishers and billed them each time. The company had high customer retention, and they were easily able to create annual and multiyear service contracts, with add-on options such as sprinkler and smoke alarm inspections for their commercial and homeowner clients. Their customers felt like they received more value from the business, and the business received a higher sale value.

Recurring revenue is a huge draw for buyers, so many companies have come up with creative ways of generating it. Many bookkeeping companies charge by the hour or by a monthly retainer, but one savvy owner created a membership model. She offered members up to ten hours of work every month for a flat rate of $500. They could then purchase additional hours at a reduced rate of $45 per hour. The agreement renewed automatically every year unless the client took action. When she transferred her customers to this new structure, she also made sure the contracts were assignable. While many bookkeeping companies are hard to sell or result in poor deal structures for the seller, she received full value for hers because of the recurring revenue and assignable contracts.

Grey Matter Matters!

Finally, you need to protect your company's intellectual property. Buyers will sense danger if the company's most important assets aren't secure. This can come in the form of NDAs with employees, clients, and partners, non-compete agreements with employees, and formal legal devices such as patents, registered trademarks, and trade secrets.

FUTURE OPPORTUNITIES

Buyers are not looking to buy stagnant companies. They're here to make money, so they want to see a dazzling future for your company. Owners looking to sell, however, don't necessarily want to make the investment of time and resources into pursuing new opportunities. The best thing owners can do is to provide organic growth opportunities on a silver platter. Be prepared to present a growth plan: a series of realistic options for how potential buyers could grow the company. Most buyers actually find this quite fun. They get to explain all the crazy ideas they've had for their company. If you believe your current model is capped on growth, you need to consider how a new owner should proceed.

Drop the Ego, Bro

You've spent years running your company, and you may justifiably feel you're pretty good at it. In that time, no doubt you've explored a number of marketing and growth strategies, some that worked and some that didn't. But when you're in meetings with the buyer, you need to put a happy face on all of this. If you were young and excited and ready to dive into this company, how would you go about it?

Sellers often talk themselves into corners during meetings with buyers. Sometimes it's a result of the owner being burned out and feeling frustrated with the company. In other cases, the owner feels attacked when the buyer questions them about past decisions. The buyer isn't trying to be critical, but rather is just trying to learn from your expertise and understand where the opportunities are. In one buyer-seller meeting, the buyer asked why the seller hadn't developed an online store to sell the company's wares. The seller responded, "Oh, I tried online. It doesn't work." The seller assumed that because he couldn't make it work, no one could—and it was pure ego. The more likely reality is that the seller probably just wasn't very good at it. Instead, the seller could have said, "You know, I tried online once, but I don't think I had enough understanding of the marketing and technology to make it work. I think there's a lot of opportunity there for you." Buyers like it when a seller hasn't run down every avenue in search of efficiency and growth. They want to believe there's room to grow in the long term, and some low-hanging fruit they can reach along the way. Be willing to admit your own limitations in running the company. Remember, you're selling a product you want them to buy.

Get the buyer excited about what could happen with this business! Explore everything we've covered in this chapter, such as improved marketing strategies, new customer segments and industries, and expanded product lines. Even if it's a strategy you tried (or failed!), consider how you might have done it better. A company's valuation is based on current financial status, but you can sometimes justify a higher valuation or multiple when an opportunity is particularly intriguing and available.

EXPANDING YOUR COMPANY'S WAISTLINE

Most buyers want to see at least 20 percent growth year over year. If you're one year out from selling your company, you may want to actively pursue smaller-scale opportunities, while creating plans for larger opportunities that could entice buyers. If you're two to three years out from selling, you can explore more substantial growth ideas. It may cost some money to bring them to fruition, but they can grow the value of your company significantly. Additionally, because you're still relatively far from selling, you'll have some time to reap the benefits of your hard work and recoup some of your costs.

As a result, there are times when it can be wise to make some investment into a new opportunity. A thought leader had developed a successful business speaking to audiences, conducting seminars, and coaching business leaders. Recently, he'd also started coaching other business speakers, and thought there was considerable opportunity in the space. He knew he wanted to sell the company at some point in the next five years, and understood he needed to keep growing the company and design a future path for the subsequent owner. He decided to start building out an online course that would train business speakers. He didn't want to fund the whole buildout himself, so he decided to focus on quality of content rather than production value. It allowed him to build the course relatively inexpensively, while generating recurring revenue and attracting a national audience he wouldn't have had access to otherwise. Originally, he planned to ask for a price of 3x SDE (seller's discretionary earnings), but with the framework of the new course in place and profitability up, his broker successfully sought a price in the range of 3.5x to 4x SDE.

The other method of expansion is via acquisition. We've covered that 80 percent of companies listed for sale don't sell. Think about the opportunities that lie in those companies! Some in that 80 percent may be so desperate to sell that you could get a fabulous bargain. Buying other companies, whether competitors, complementary service providers, or a new market space altogether, can be a faster, more efficient way to mature a company or extend into new areas. Evaluate the landscape of your industry. Where does the market seem to be going? What changes do you anticipate? What capabilities would position your company to be at the forefront of the sector in the future? Then see what companies (and their employees) have what you lack, even if they're not quite inside your industry. Don't try to incorporate anything too large, particularly if you're within two years of selling. Instead, investigate their customer lists or physical assets you could purchase for just a few thousand dollars. See Chapter 6 for more information about the opportunities in acquisitions.

KEY TAKEAWAYS:

- Staging your company—both physically and virtually—is important. Take pride in your business' outward presentation and the story it tells.
- Online reviews are not going away. Make sure your online presence reflects your business in the best possible light.
- Buyers want growth! Be prepared to explain the growth potential buyers could achieve without significant additional investment.

TO DO NOW:

- Tackle your company's website and online reviews, and examine your social media presence. Make sure they are clean, focused, and appropriate.
- Start documenting growth opportunities for the business. If you are far enough out from sale, evaluate potential investments and acquisitions you could make.
- Read John Spence's book *Awesomely Simple: Essential Business Strategies for Turning Ideas into Action*. His six key strategies will help you frame the merits of your business to the buyer.

CHAPTER 5

Financials

When you're teaching your baby (well, teenager) to drive, you need to make sure they understand some fundamentals first, such as the rules of the road and the basic functioning of the car. They need to know when and how to use a blinker, where to look before turning, and how to turn the wheel. There's a similar task when rearing your business baby: financials.

Many business owners don't understand the financials of their company at all. As soon as the discussion turns to money, their eyes glaze over and they say, "My accountant does all that." And if they're not bored of the topic, they're scared of it. These owners need to change the way they think about the numbers in their businesses.

NUMBERS ARE EMPOWERING, NOT FRIGHTENING

Financials are incredibly important, but they don't have to be intimidating. Whatever your negative feelings towards financials, set aside your emotions. Ultimately, financials are scorecards that measure performance. Many owners already keep scorecards, such as revenue, sales prospects, marketing conversion rates, and customer satisfaction ratings. Financial statements are just another type of scorecard, this one measuring the value of the company.

Understanding the numbers gives you ownership over the entire business sale process. They're what business brokers use to value the business, what buyers use to determine the price they'll pay, and what banks use to calculate whether they'll approve a loan. These issues are exactly what prevent most companies from selling. They're also the most important elements in determining whether and how much cash you receive at the closing table. If you can learn to appreciate the numbers, you can make more accurate predictions and better prioritize your actions.

Don't Do It Alone . . . or Perhaps at All

For a few owners, however, keeping a tight fist on finances is a point of pride. They don't want to pay someone else to do a task they can do themselves, or don't want to invest in the computer software that would bring their books into the twenty-first century. This is a shortsighted view that probably costs considerably more than it saves. You can find qualified bookkeepers who charge as little as $50 per hour. As an owner, your time is probably worth far more than that. Do the math: you're probably losing money by doing the financials yourself. Worse, you're probably doing them incorrectly and infrequently.

When a company goes on the market, the owner should not be the one managing the books, and they certainly shouldn't be done by hand. For owners who dislike finances, you're already a step ahead. You recognize bean counting isn't your strength, and you're comfortable outsourcing the job. Fully outsourcing accounting functions will save you time and ensure the books are done correctly. At the very least, you need to create a system (using computer software!) with checks and balances, where a bookkeeper (again, not you!) is complemented by an outside accountant. This will widen your buyer pool by reducing risk to the new buyer. It also will save time in the sales process because the buyer will not feel as compelled to examine your books with a fine-tooth comb if you have a reputable accounting firm confirming your internal bookkeeping. Optics matter here; when buyers see sloppy books, they'll wonder what else in the company is disorganized and mismanaged.

At the end of the day, business is about making money. Crass? Maybe. Reality? Absolutely. No matter your passion for the industry, you wouldn't have continued running the company if it hadn't provided enough for you and your family. Similarly, buyers aren't searching for failing entities without potential. You need to make it easy for buyers to see what a great company you have. To make your company appealing, you need to make the financials as clean and attractive as possible, and you're probably better off allowing an expert to do it for you.

WHY FINANCIALS MATTER

The best outcome for a seller is to walk away at closing with as much cash as possible. This is highly unlikely to happen if your financials are not in order. Most business sale transactions involve bank loans, and banks view businesses only in terms of their finances. Your business baby is just a number to them, so it's your responsibility to make it as attractive a number as possible.

As mentioned, finances are like the scorecard for the business, and ultimately will make or break the deal. The two main financial documents—the balance sheet and income statement—are the easiest and fastest ways to determine the health of a company. In fact, they're likely the very first thing a buyer will look at during due diligence. The documents don't need to be the perfect product a CPA might produce, but they should be clean and consistent from year to year. Nothing will make a buyer walk away faster than disorganized accounting.

As you dig into the financial nuances of your company as you prepare to sell, you'll start to recognize areas of weakness and strength. If you don't feel you can make these assessments yourself, you have a CPA and a business broker ready to help! Take this opportunity to make changes that will put your company in a better financial position and strengthen its outlook. Identify places where the company could grow, and be prepared to share this information with a potential buyer during due diligence. Examining and understanding your books will make your company stronger and improve your ability to market the business.

Messy financial documents will absolutely impact the price you're able to get for your business. When your books aren't neat or updated, the value of your business is obscured. Further, it raises a red flag for the buyer. If the books aren't tidy, what else in the business is untidy? The buyer views this as a risk, and if they don't walk away, they will at least want a lower price. Messy books may also cause a bank to refuse a loan application. Banks will not look favorably on your business baby when the one thing they examine—the financials—are sloppy. Ultimately, the deal may have to rely heavily on seller financing, which increases the risk to the owner and reduces the cash they walk away with at closing.

Make sure you don't put off the inevitable. One business owner listed her company for sale. The business was performing well and it was the right time of year, so she found a buyer and got a contract quickly. But the seller had been so busy running her company that she hadn't been able to reconcile her books for the past three years. During due diligence, the buyer discovered the backlog and was shocked. Once she realized the gravity of the situation, the seller stayed up seventy-two hours straight to get her financials in order. Her heroics saved the deal, but certainly wreaked havoc on her sleep.

Technicalities and Taxes

At some point, you may have to choose between accrual accounting and cash accounting. Basically, accrual accounting reports revenue and expenses when they occur, rather than when they are paid, while cash accounting reports revenue and expenses when they are actually paid. There are pros and cons to each, and you should discuss them with your financial professional. Ultimately, however, I strongly recommend accrual accounting for your bookkeeping, as this is what buyers and bankers will expect in the sales process. It may require some initial investment of time and resources into your bookkeeping, and may even cause you a temporary uptick in taxes (although there is a method that enables you to use accrual accounting in your bookkeeping but still file your taxes on a cash basis). If the goal is to sell your business for the most value possible, accrual accounting is the best way to go.

And if you haven't, pay your taxes. It may sound obvious, but taxes can get out of control quickly. Additionally, if you don't do long-term planning with a tax professional who is experienced with small business owners, you will regret it. Taxes follow the business rather than the business owner, so they're a huge risk for buyers. There are so many different types of taxes you could be subject to (federal and state income, payroll, sales, real estate, personal property, excise, gross receipts, franchise, capital gains . . .), and a failure to pay any one of them could fundamentally shift the financial picture of your company—and ultimately kill a deal.

If you're in a tax situation, it doesn't mean you can't sell your business. You do, however, need to be up front with the buyer. You also need to have a plan to pay off what you owe either before or using the proceeds from closing. And make sure you're aware of any pending actions against you before you put your company on the market. The owner of a fitness studio invited a potential buyer to sit in on a popular class. Right in the middle of the session, the county sheriff arrived, cleared the building, and locked the front door. He then posted a sign that the business was being shut down due to chronic unpaid sales taxes. Needless to say, the buyer did not move forward with the deal.

THE MAIN FINANCIAL DOCUMENTS

During due diligence, a buyer will always ask for two main financial documents—the balance sheet and income statement—as well as tax returns and bank statements. Together, the balance sheet and income statement explain the overall financial status of your company. All four documents need to tie together: if you show $200,000 of earnings on your income statement, that same number should be reflected on your balance sheet and tax return. The more cohesive these documents, the stronger your argument for a solid sales price.

Before you take your company to market, you should have the last three years of these documents in pristine condition, as well as up-to-date numbers for the current year. Best practice is to close your books and have financial reports ready every month. At a bare minimum, you can do this quarterly, but buyers and banks will look less favorably on this. If you have the time and resources, go back further than three years. If your industry is susceptible to market dips or recessions or if a bank is financing the transaction, you'll likely be required to do so anyway. Start working on these documents with your outside accountant as soon as possible. Also, notify your outside accountant that you'll be selling the business (making sure they understand the importance of confidentiality). They need to be prepared to produce documents in short order, and not doing so could impact your ability to close the deal.

Balance Sheet

The balance sheet is like a snapshot of your company: it lays out the company's assets, liabilities, and shareholder equity at a specific moment in time. Buyers will use the balance sheet to understand your ownership structure, calculate various evaluation measurements, and see what assets and liabilities are needed to run the business. Buyers also use it to identify how much working capital they'll need to bring into the business to keep the company running. Now is the time to clean up any past tax liabilities that would otherwise show up on the balance sheet—remember, the cleaner these documents, the better. Make sure the balance sheet doesn't include personal assets or expenses (more on this later in the chapter).

Below is an example balance sheet, based on the financials of a real company. Notice that all assets and liabilities pertinent to running the company are included.

Sample Company Balance Sheet As of December 31, 2020	
	Total
ASSETS	
Current Assets	
Bank Accounts	
Checking Account	207,625.98
Savings	50,000.00
Total Bank Accounts	**$ 257,625.98**
Accounts Receivable	10,000.00
Inventory	50,000.00
Rent Deposit	7,500.00
Total Current Assets	**$ 325,125.98**
Fixed Assets	
Vehicles	33,668.24
Furniture Fixtures & Equipment	7,875.00
Total Fixed Assets	**$ 41,543.24**
TOTAL ASSETS	**$ 366,669.22**
LIABILITIES AND EQUITY	
Liabilities	
Current Liabilities	
Credit Card	3,264.56
Line of Credit	2,894.55
Total Current Liabilities	**$ 6,159.11**
Long-Term Liabilities	
Bank Loan	33,500.00
Loan—Owner	4,890.05
Total Long-Term Liabilities	**$ 38,390.05**

(continued on next page)

Total Liabilities	**$ 44,549.16**
Equity	
Member Draw	-134.48
Retained Earnings	217,254.54
Opening Balance Equity	5,000.00
Net Income	$ 100,000.00
Total Equity	**$ 322,120.06**
TOTAL LIABILITIES AND EQUITY	**$ 366,669.22**

Income Statement

The income statement (also called the profit and loss statement, or P&L) reports the company's financial performance over a certain period of time and explains how revenue turns into earnings. It reveals how much overhead you have and how much it costs to produce the goods you sell. The P&L also informs buyers about management efficiency, operational performance of divisions within the company, and overall company performance relative to competitors. When creating the income statement, make sure the categories you use are consistent from year to year so the buyer can get a clear sense of changes over time.

Below is an example income statement, based on the financials of a real company. Notice this P&L includes all expenses and revenues relevant to the business. It provides a clear picture without being overly detailed.

Sample Company **Profit and Loss** **January–December 2020**	
	Total
Income	
Sales	963,163.05
Total Income	**$ 963,163.05**
Cost of Goods and Service	

(continued on next page)

Billable Expense	1,489.01
Credit Card Fees	19,263.26
Contractors	674,214.14
Total Cost of Goods Sold	**$ 694,966.41**
Gross Profit	**$ 268,196.64**
Expenses	
Supplies	1,540.13
Shipping and delivery expense	113.33
Payroll (Admin)	78,000.22
Payroll Taxes (Admin)	5,850.02
Payroll Fees	1,422.00
Telephone	397.52
Advertising	50,522.91
Promotional	961.15
Insurance	2,461.61
Travel	10,690.74
Meals and Entertainment	520.69
Gifts	1,218.09
Interest Expense	520.15
Bank Charges	250.00
Legal & Professional Fees	4,000.00
Recruiting	1,459.03
Technology	7,285.06
Dues & Subscriptions	984.00
Total Expenses	**$ 168,196.65**
Net Operating Income	**$ 100,000.00**

PERSONAL EXPENSES AND TAXES

When you're trying to sell your company, it's critically important you don't use your business as a personal piggy bank. At the very least, you should eliminate personal expenses for the last year, but three years is strongly preferred. This may require you to go through your financial statements and tie up a bunch of loose ends, which can be a time-consuming, expensive proposition as you pay off debts and catch up on taxes. As with transitioning to accrual accounting, short-term pain here leads to long-term gain.

If an expense isn't essential to and reasonable for maintaining business operations at the current level, it shouldn't be included as a business expense. This is especially true if a bank is financing part of the deal—they do not want to see any personal expenses, and the business's ability to qualify for a loan may be impacted. Further, counting a personal expense as a business expense makes the company's SDE (seller's discretionary earnings) appear lower than it actually is, which will reduce the price buyers are willing to pay. You'll need to restate your financial documents after you've made these adjustments, called add-backs. The longer you've been maintaining clean books, the better: just about every owner will have add-backs, but having an excessive number of them can reflect poorly on your management. And fear not: just because you remove your personal expenditures from your company's books doesn't necessarily mean you'll lose the tax savings you gained from putting them there in the first place. You can create a holding company that services the operating entity and still allows you to use tax write-offs. Ask your accountant about these strategies.

Alas, some owners still take the "business-as-piggy-bank" concept to the extreme. A distribution company was for sale. It was a large, successful company that had provided the owner with a luxurious lifestyle. Before taking the company to market, his business broker noticed the profit margins were lower than those of most comparable distribution companies, and was struck by how high the expenses in certain categories were. Upon closer examination, the broker discovered the owner had been running personal expenses through the business for years and hiding them in various categories of the P&L. The business paid for, among other things, four Lamborghinis, ten ATV four wheelers, and a shockingly expensive divorce. There were literally millions of dollars of personal expenses on the business books, and the company was basically unsellable despite its profitability and growth potential.

Other owners go to great lengths to shield their income from taxes. I've known of business owners who keep one set of books that accounts for the credit card transactions they do, and another set of books for the cash transactions—and only show the IRS the credit card version. Some owners with all cash businesses completely falsify their books. Companies with clearly fictional books are not sellable. No (honest) buyer would touch them with a ten-foot pole for fear of being taken advantage of, and for fear of what the government might do if they found out. And even if such a seller found a buyer comfortable playing fast and loose with the law, the owner still wouldn't get full value for the company. First, it would be difficult to establish an accurate value for the company. Second, the buyer would want to be compensated with a lower sales price in exchange for taking on additional risk.

Honesty Is Still the Best Policy

Being dishonest is, quite literally, not worth it. If you're shielding money from Uncle Sam by hiding it in the company, you'll get a lower price for the company when you sell. If you pay Uncle Sam up front, you'll get more money upon selling. In fact, every dollar that you assign correctly to the bottom line of your company will get you at least two to three additional dollars in sale value. Ultimately, that's worth a lot more than the few cents of taxes you're saving by shielding the assets in the company.

Besides, there are plenty of ways for owners to pay themselves with methods the IRS and banks find legitimate while still reducing their tax liability and maintaining the value of their company. For example, owners can max out 401(k) contributions that will save money for the future and protect their families. Additionally, if you have a spouse that works in the business, you can max out their retirement savings as well. The advantage of these methods—beyond their legality—is that they won't hurt you when it comes to sales price and bank financing. Get your financial planner and CPA involved before you put your company on the market.

THE TIME TO START IS NOW

For many owners, untangling the web of years of financial history sounds about as enticing as death by a thousand paper cuts. To keep your sanity, start small. From today onward, have crystal-clean books. Then start with last year, and work with your CPA to clean out just that one year. If necessary, restate your tax returns for that year. Soon you'll be ready for the prior year, and so on. If your company has multiple locations, you need separate sets of books for each of them (even if you only file one tax return). The process will be painful, but you'll congratulate yourself when you get a higher sales price and walk away with a lot more cash in your pocket when you close.

To further increase the value of your company, you can either increase revenue or reduce expenses. Check out Chapter 8 for the exact steps you need to take, and when you need to take them.

KEY TAKEAWAYS:

- Financial management is key to a successful business sale.
- Owners should outsource their accounting in order to establish a system with checks and balances.
- Cleaning your books of personal and non-essential business expenses will maximize SDE, and thereby get you a better price for your company.

TO DO NOW:

- Start keeping clean and updated books and records today, and maintain them from here on out. If you don't have one, hire a bookkeeper and an outside accountant to manage the books.
- Set a goal to have completed financial reports on a monthly basis. If that is too much, start with quarterly. If you must, set a meeting with an accountability partner to keep you on track.
- Once you have a good process in place, go back and restate financials for the past three years. This is especially important if there were significant issues in the business or if you plan on selling in the next twelve months.

CHAPTER 6

Preparation Timeline to Increase the Value of Your Business

You may believe you have the most beautiful business baby in the world. But even model babies wear makeup and go through dozens of pictures to get the perfect shot. It takes time to prepare your company for sale. Of course, the best thing you can do to help your company get listed and sell as fast as possible is to be prepared for sale at any time. Realistically, however, that isn't likely to happen. Most entrepreneurs wake up one day and decide they're finished. If you want to create the most value in your sale and increase the likelihood it goes through, your best bet is to put at least a few items in place as soon as possible.

This chapter offers a list of must-do activities based on how long you have before you want to list the company for sale. But remember, even after you list the company for sale, you're still likely six to twelve months away from closing a deal. Also understand that these lists are not comprehensive; rather, they're the bare minimum you can do and still set your company up for sales success. This chapter is meant to help you prioritize the most critical actions—it's not a shortcut to maximized value.

These lists build on each other. So if you have one year until you put your company up for sale, first do the items listed under "Only Six Months Until Listing," and then move on to the "One to Two Years Until Listing" items. And if you have two or more years, do everything from the first two lists before you begin the third list.

In creating these preparation timelines, I'm making a few assumptions about your company. The first assumption is that your company is profitable. If it's not, you'll only be able to sell your business for a percentage of the assets. Basically, until your company is profitable, you're conducting a fire sale. If it's at all possible to delay the sale, take the time to get the business into the black.

Second, I'm assuming you have outside advisors. You should consider talking to a business broker, and you need an outside accountant. Above all, you must have a business transactions lawyer and a tax advisor, both of whom are experienced in small business sales. Without them, you will pay far more in taxes and legal fees in the long run.

The third caveat is more strong advice than assumption, but it can't be emphasized enough: No matter how long you have until putting your company on the market, you should engage in a structured sales preparation process, such as Exit Factor's Prep to Sell course. Selling a business is very different from running one. Without a systematic approach, you're basically guaranteed to leave money on the table, all while wasting time and accumulating stress.

ONLY SIX MONTHS UNTIL LISTING

Having only six months until you put your company on the market is not ideal, but it can be done. If this is your goal, you need to set aside time in your calendar to work on these steps—and then you need to stick to that schedule. Done properly, you can complete your preparatory work in just one to two hours per week. Your focus, after all, must be on running the business profitably and effectively.

To be clear, you can't do this on your own. You'll need to lean on your internal team to get everything done. Make sure you don't tell them you're selling—see Chapters 2 and 3 for more on the importance of confidentiality—but use their skills by setting goals for them that will help you accomplish what needs to get done. And of course, remember that your sales advisory team should include an outside accountant.

If you're listing your company in six months, here are your top priorities:

1. Financial Cleanup

First and foremost, you need to get your books in order. You need at least one, but preferably three, years of white glove inspection-ready documents. Recall from Chapter 5 that the two main financial documents are the balance sheet and income statement. You should also be prepared with those years' tax returns. Inconsistencies in these documents will cause the biggest devaluation, so you need to get all this information in sync. Revenue and expenses must be logged into the appropriate categories, and those categories must be consistent over time. All the documents should match up and reflect the same numbers. Your personal expenses need to be gone from the records.

This financial cleanup is the single most important thing you will do to prepare your company for sale. If you're in an absolute worst-case scenario and only have time for one thing, this is that thing (but please avoid that scenario!).

2. Document Your Role as Owner

In Chapter 3, we cover why it's important for sellers to make themselves as irrelevant as possible to the day-to-day running of the business. If you're like most owners, however, you won't be able to totally remove yourself in just six months. Therefore, it's particularly important to document exactly what you do.

The day after your sale closes, the buyer will have to run the company on their own. What's the first thing they need to do? What are your daily, weekly, monthly, quarterly, and annual rhythms? What do you do that no one else knows how or is willing to do? Many of these items are so ingrained in an owner's head that they don't think about or mention them—leaving the new owner with an impossible learning curve. Write it all down for them.

Of course, if you have time, you should train someone on your staff to do as much of this work as possible. At the very least, describe how you would train a staff member, or identify someone outside of the company who could do the job.

The more thoroughly you document your processes, the easier the transition will be for the buyer. It will also reiterate to the buyer what a strong operational understanding you have of the company, which lends credibility as you answer their questions and enter negotiations.

3. Clean Up the Company's Reputation

With only six months until taking your company to market, you need to focus on fundamentals and obvious problems. Bad online reviews of your company can be a huge eyesore and give buyers all kinds of doubts. You need to undergo an online facelift to eliminate major blemishes.

First, take a deep breath. Then, respond publicly to the negative reviews—in a calm, solicitous, non-defensive tone. State that you're sorry there's been a problem, and that you'll connect with them privately to resolve the issue. In such a short amount of time, you may not be able to respond to every negative comment or totally turn around your overall rating. Still, spending a few minutes each week for six months can add up, and you'll get through a lot of them. As we covered in Chapter 4, this kind of outreach has an amazingly high success rate in getting the reviewer to remove or improve the original review.

Second, respond to the positive reviews. Thank your customers and say how much you like working with them. Further, don't be shy about drumming up more positive reviews. Happy customers are usually glad to post online.

Finally, remember that *you* are not your business. The next owner won't be able to rely on your charisma and relationships to draw in customers or make sales, so don't present the company that way. You probably won't have time for a full rebranding, but you can at least remove yourself from marketing materials and reduce your presence on the company website. Make everything about the company and the team as a whole, and not about you as the owner.

ONE TO TWO YEARS UNTIL LISTING

If you know you're going to sell, this is the ideal time to start your preparatory work. It's enough time to tidy up your operations and make sure you're in a strong position to sell, although it's probably not enough time to make longer-term investments of time or money into expanding the business. To prepare to list your company for sale in one to two years, complete the list above, and then tackle these:

4. Reduce Your Operational Role in the Business

In this scenario, you can do more than just document your role in the company. With more time, you can take an actual step back from your responsibilities. The goal is to become a hands-off owner, instead of an operational employee.

Make a list of all you do and consider how you might delegate those tasks. Which duties can be taken over by staff? Who on your team is the most equipped to handle each? Will any of them require training? Consider what should be done by outside experts. Explore computer software options, which might do the job more efficiently than any human. Chapter 3 has more information on how to prepare for this transition.

Reducing your role is particularly important in terms of sales and customer service. If you're involved in a customer-facing activity at any point in the process, transition someone else into that role. You want your customers to do business with your company, not with you. A personal touch from the owner may have been an effective way to start and grow your company, but it's no way to run a company that's for sale. One of a buyer's biggest concerns is that customers will disappear when you do, so they perceive more risk when owners interact closely with customers. The challenge is that you can't really hire a third party to do customer service. Instead, you'll need to find someone in your company who can play the part. Identify the necessary skills in your team and start now on training them and involving them in the process.

5. Review and Update Assignment Clauses in Legal Agreements

The next step is to examine all the company's contracts and determine whether they're assignable to a new owner. This is an important way to reduce risk for a potential buyer. On the first day, the new owner doesn't want to have to enter negotiations just to make sure the company can keep operating.

Review contracts related to your lease, employees, customers, vendors, and anything else you've signed. You'll need at least a year to do this: Most of these contracts are probably on one-year terms, and the most appropriate time to make these changes is during regular contract renewal. The next time you enter negotiations to re-up any contract, you'll be ready to add or adjust assignment clauses without causing any alarm. Also make sure all the contracts are with the company, and not with you.

6. Document Key Processes

Hopefully as you've reduced your role from operator to owner (as discussed in Chapter 3), you've also reduced the need to explain your responsibilities in writing. Instead, document key processes throughout the business. Document your role as an owner (now minimized!), recruiting and onboarding, and the entire sales process, from identifying new potential customers through delivering the product or service. Having clear standards and procedures reduces the risk to the buyer and can even increase the valuation. It can also lessen your involvement in any transition period.

You don't have to create a painstakingly detailed 500-page manual; even just a list of bullet points for each process is great. It proves to the buyer that you have a full grasp of the entire company's functioning and that there are organized procedures in place. Such a list is also an opportunity to make sure your employees are following each process as they should, while giving them the autonomy to make it work for them. And if you find things need adjustment, seize the moment to implement changes.

Be aware that many potential buyers will mystery shop the business and pose as a customer to see how things are done. You can be sure they'll find the holes in the process. So make sure what you document is actually what is being done, and that what is being done is the right thing!

TWO YEARS OR MORE UNTIL LISTING

When you have two or more years until you plan to list your company for sale, you have the time to clean things up and make progress on longer-term growth. You'll focus on how to grow revenue, and more importantly, how to increase profitability.

With so much time until taking your business to market, complete all six steps above, and then invest time and money on the following:

7. Increase Margins and Reduce Costs

A key goal is to increase margins and reduce costs. Implementing these improvements amplifies the impact of subsequent growth strategies. There are many ways to go about this, but one of the most effective ways of increasing margins is to reduce the cost of delivering your good or service (often called COGS, or cost of goods sold). Find new, less expensive vendors or renegotiate existing relationships (and make sure any new contracts are assignable).

You can also look to reduce operational expenses and overhead. These kinds of changes can take time, so proceed with caution. One company needed to increase margins and decided to do so by reducing commission percentages to their sales team. In exchange, however, they found other ways to give value to those employees, like increased vacation time and more professional development opportunities. Instead of making the changes immediately, they rolled out the changes slowly over the course of the year. At the end of the transition period, the company achieved their goal, and almost every single member of the sales team actually thanked the owner for making the change. Contrast that to a different company that made the same exact changes, but enacted them almost overnight. They lost 80 percent of their sales team in the first week!

8. Plan for Organic Growth

Larger companies get higher sales prices, so if you're selling your business, you want it to be as large as possible! As with improving margins and reducing costs above, there are lots of ways to increase revenue. Increase your customer base by seeking customers from varying sources, industries, and sizes. Extend your product lines by designing products and services of varying sizes, creating additional subscription services, or combining a product with a service. Add new revenue streams such as affiliate or referral partnerships or joint ventures. Chapters 3 and 4 cover all these options in more detail. If your sales team needs help developing process and technique, read *The Sales Playbook for Hyper Sales Growth* by Jack Daly and Dan Larson. Remember, however, that the metric you need to focus on is profit. Increasing revenue won't help you at all if your profits are stagnant or declining.

9. Consider Growth Through Acquisition

Now that you know so much about how to sell a company, let's return to a sobering statistic: 80 percent of businesses never sell. But this time, instead of letting it scare you, use that knowledge to your advantage! There are tons of opportunities to buy companies for less than they're worth, and this can be a terrific way to expand your company. You also get an instant influx of skilled staff, regional impact, and new customers.

Selling a company takes time, but buying a company can be done in as little as three to six months. In fact, when the company is already on the market and the buyer is paying cash, I've seen deals close in thirty days! Obviously this is easier (and faster) said than done. If you're trying to buy out a competitor, you may have to cater to them for years. If the company you want to buy isn't on the market, it can add months to the process. Using bank financing adds 30 to 60 days to the process. And ultimately, the biggest challenge is integrating the new business into your existing company.

Still, valuations are determined by the quantity and quality of earnings (profit!), and buying a company can be an efficient way to grow both. Buyers are willing to pay higher multiples for higher earnings. It makes sense: buyers are nervous about taking over a company and dropping the ball. The higher the revenue, the more cushion they have if they make a mistake. For example, if the company has $50,000 in net profit, the new owner basically only has room for one screwup before they're in the red. But if the company has $500,000 in net profit, the owner can afford a couple mistakes before they're in real trouble.

Just like determining the rate of income tax you pay, there are certain valuation tripping points that can trigger higher multiples. These usually happen at half million-dollar increments. So if you grow your company from $200,000 to $500,000 in net profit, you can go from a 2x multiple to a 4x multiple on the sale. The closer you are to one of these half million-dollar increments, the more you should consider an acquisition that would get you over the edge.

Be careful not to bite off more than you can chew. The closer you are to going to market, the smaller the acquisition should be. If you only have two years, choose a smaller company (aim for a company about one quarter of your size) in a similar industry. You can always buy a more sizable company later. With enough time, you could even acquire a company larger than your own, but these transactions are rare, and doing so certainly shouldn't be your first time acquiring a company.

If acquisitions really make you nervous, other acquisition-like strategies can be extremely efficient. You can buy a defunct business for a few thousand dollars. If it's a company in your industry, this will gain you their entire customer list for pennies on the dollar of what it would cost you to acquire those names via traditional marketing. You could even buy a failed company's Facebook page for a few hundred dollars. Get creative and see what might be of value to you!

CHAPTER 7

Top Ten Questions from Sellers

Deciding to sell your baby is among the most significant decisions an owner will ever make. You'll have a million thoughts and questions running around your head. Here are the answers to the most frequent questions my brokers and I get from business owners who are deciding whether to sell their companies.

1. Is my company even sellable?

Many owners wrongly believe they have a unicorn on their hands that will surely bring them tens of millions of dollars upon sale. But a surprising number of owners alternatively (and wrongly) believe no one would have any interest in buying their company. In fact, almost every company is sellable in one way or another. Most of the time, you can sell the whole kit and caboodle to one buyer. In a few situations, you'll only be able to sell the assets, such as equipment, customer list, or website. You should never, ever assume the company isn't worth anything. At worst, something is better than nothing, right? You should avoid just shutting down the company and walking way, because then you're guaranteed to get no value at all. A plumber, who assumed his company wasn't sellable, happened to meet a broker at a holiday party. The broker convinced him to get his company valuated, and it turned out it was worth $1.4 million. It totally changed the trajectory of his life. Whatever your situation, your broker can help you explore the best possible outcomes and get you the most value. It's always worth the conversation, and there's no risk to you to find out! Review Chapter 1 for more information on valuing a business and how you'll get paid.

2. How much time will it take to sell the company?

There are two elements to this question: how much of the owner's time it will take to sell, and how long it will be between deciding to sell and closing the deal. I can almost guarantee you'll underestimate both. First, let's discuss the owner's time. Selling a company is like having an additional full-time job. That's why it's so important to have outsourced processes, external advisors, and a business broker. There's just no way you can do it all on your own, especially when your most important job needs to be keeping your company running profitably. With the proper support in place (and some self-discipline), however, you can do all the prep work you need to do by dedicating two to three hours per week to the effort.

Next is the issue of the overall length of time it takes to sell. It will take you at least—at least!—six months to prepare your company for sale, but preferably you'll have a year—even two!—to do all the prep work necessary. Once you take the company to market, the national average is eight and a half months before you find a buyer and close the deal. Remember that even once you find a buyer, half of all deals still die during due diligence. During the (on average) eight and a half months between listing and closing, you'll come to terms with the buyer, ensure bank financing is in line, and get everything in order for closing. That eight and a half months will also include the thirty days you'll need to close the deal, as well as the sixty days you'll need if there's bank financing involved. Chapter 2 has more information on the timeline, and Chapter 8 gives a list of priority action items depending on how long you have to prepare your company for listing.

Above all, you need to start planning now. The very first moment exiting your company crosses your mind, start the planning process, because you needed to start planning *yesterday*. Get things in order now, before you mentally check out or get exhausted from burnout. Some sellers leave money on the table; they're so desperate to escape their company that they become more interested in getting away than in getting the most value. And even if you don't have any intention to walk away for decades, you don't know what life will bring your way. As explained in Chapter 1, you need to have ever-ready exit options that can be executed quickly. You must protect yourself. If you don't, you could be forced to take a lower price in an emergency situation where you need money the most.

3. How much will it cost to sell?

There is some cost involved in selling your company. You'll need to pay the advisors you bring on. Brokers typically get a commission on the sale (sometimes they're called "success-based fees"), but they work on contingency, meaning they only get paid if you sell. Bringing in an outside accountant may be a new expense, but it's one you should have anyway. Attorneys usually work for an hourly rate. While you certainly don't need to spring for a rainmaking attorney at an elite firm, a general practitioner also will not do. You need a lawyer specifically experienced in small business transactions. Financial advisors often collect a management fee based on the assets under management. Your business broker likely has a list of trusted advisors they've worked with in the past who are talented and reasonably priced. Chapter 2 has more details on what to expect when paying your advisors.

Most business sales are referred to as "cash free, debt free" deals. This means the seller gets to keep the cash sitting in the business' bank account, but the seller is also responsible for paying off any debt the company has been carrying. The money for the debt the seller pays off will come either from the cash in the business' bank account, or from the cash received from the sale of the company.

Last but certainly not least, there are taxes. It's shocking, the number of sellers who totally (conveniently?) forget they will have to pay tax on this transaction. Now, if you enjoy paying more than your fair share in taxes, great! Carry on as you will, and don't worry about working with a financial advisor. But if you're not looking to give the government more than necessary, read on. Depending on how well (and how far in advance) you've planned and on how you structure the deal, the transaction can be taxed at a capital gains rate, at the ordinary income rate, or with a combination of both (or even not at all! Really! Talk to your tax advisor.). This is why you need a great team including an attorney, financial advisor, and CPA who are experienced in business sales. They can save you *hundreds of thousands of dollars*. See Chapter 2 for tips on how to choose the right advisors.

4. How much will I get for my company?

The company's valuation is a pain point for many owners. This business is their baby, and as far as they're concerned, their baby is beautiful and special and has tons of potential. Unfortunately, your company is almost certainly not worth what you think it should be. Emotionally prepare yourself now for the letdown: the buyer is not going to think your baby is as beautiful as you think it is.

The value of your company is based strictly on its financials, not on its potential. Once the buyer determines a valuation for your company, they pay a certain multiple based on that number. Generally for small businesses, SDE (seller's discretionary earnings) determines valuation. For companies under $10 million, the average multiple is 2.4. Chapter 1 covers business valuation, and Chapter 5 has more information on financials.

5. Will I get paid for my inventory, equipment, and other assets? What about my ideas?

Well, yes, you will get paid for the inventory, equipment, and other assets, but not as you might imagine. Their value is built into the price of the company. Selling a business is like selling a cash flow machine. The assets and equipment are integral parts of the machine, so they're sold as a single unit. This is also true of patents that are essential to the business. So in most cases, you won't get paid separately for them. (In some cases, patents that aren't essential to the business can be sold separately. Check with your broker.)

Unfortunately, you won't get any money for your ideas. Lots of sellers say they have, for example, a brilliant new marketing scheme guaranteed to bring in a whole new segment of clients. Some have a vast network of connections they'll introduce the buyer to. Many owners are disappointed when they hear they won't get any extra money from the buyer for these resources. Still, once you're protected by an NDA, you should share the ideas and connections with the buyer! You're trying to prove your company still has lots of upside and is worth the investment the buyer is making. Your marketing idea and established network are perfect examples of why that's true. Sharing them will build credibility and rapport with the buyer.

6. What if someone involved is a bad actor?

Lots of buyers worry about the potential for someone involved in the sales transaction to have nefarious intentions. What if someone poses as a buyer just to get access to your customer list, copy your unique sales process, or steal something else valuable? Think of it like the risk of your house getting robbed. If someone is really, really motivated to get in and take something, there may not be a lot you can do about it. But you can take precautionary measures to reduce the likelihood of it happening and the impact it would have.

This is exactly why you should engage a business broker to guide you through the sales process and take your company to market. Brokers know how to market a company confidentially, and can weed out unserious, or worse, malicious buyers. Brokers are prepared with NDAs (non-disclosure agreements) and can sniff out signs of deceit. A broker will have multiple evaluative steps for the buyer to pass through before they ever get near you. Plus, brokers save you a ton of time by marketing your company efficiently, tapping into their network, and fielding inquiries about your company that you'd otherwise have to do by yourself.

7. Do I have to sign a non-compete agreement when I sell?

Almost all buyers ask sellers to sign non-compete agreements guaranteeing the seller will not start a new company that would attract the employees and customers away from the original company. When an employee signs a non-compete agreement with their company, the agreements often are not enforceable in court. When a seller signs a non-compete agreement with a buyer, however, they usually are enforceable in court. Now, some sellers are so anxious to be out of the business that they would happily sign non-compete agreements that apply to the entire universe until the end of time. If so, sign away!

Other sellers are less sure of their future plans, or hesitate to sign such a document. If the buyer insists on a non-compete, don't let that be the reason the deal falls through. By law, non-compete agreements must be reasonable, although that definition varies by state and by the specifics of the deal. If you're selling a nail salon, a reasonable non-compete might prevent you from opening another salon within five miles of the original. If you're selling a regional chain of nail salons, a reasonable non-compete might prevent you from opening a store within a multi-state area. It's limiting, but doesn't entirely ban you from opening another salon as long as it's far enough away. Further, most non-competes can only last a few years. Even if you want to get back in the business eventually, you're probably selling because you want a break. Two or three years will absolutely fly by, and at the end of it, you still might not be ready to get back in the rat race. Whatever you decide, your broker and attorney will help you navigate this part of the conversation with the buyer. Resistance by a seller to sign a non-compete agreement can be a big red flag to buyers, and easily kill a deal.

8. Do I need advisors with experience in my industry?

It's not necessary to have advisors—brokers, attorneys, financial advisors—with business sales experience in your particular industry. The important qualification is that they're active and experienced in deals of your size and in your geographic region. Industry, however, usually doesn't matter. In fact, it's often to the seller's benefit to have advisors with business sales experience in a variety of industries. Advisors with a wider breadth of experience can use creative deal structures and negotiation techniques that may be unusual in your industry, but highly effective. For example, deals in the tech and e-commerce space often use an earn out structure. A tech industry specialist may tell you that earn outs "are just how deals are done here," but it's simply not true. I've seen a number of "generalist" brokers craft a variety of different deal structures in the tech space, with fabulous results for buyers and sellers. The added advantage of generalist advisors is that they have access to a wider pool of buyers, which helps you sell for the best price possible. Check out Chapter 2 for more information on each type of advisor you need and how to pick a good one.

Finally, at the risk of sounding like a broken record, let me emphasize an important point one more time: you must have a business transactions attorney! Any other kind of specialist, even your regular business attorney, will not do. It's got to be a business transactions attorney. And for the love of everything sacred, *don't* hire a litigator!

9. How do I negotiate the best deal for myself?

The important thing to remember about negotiating the sale of your company is that you don't need to win every point—you just need to win the ones that matter to you. Don't approach negotiations like a zero-sum game. It's not a war where the side with the most battle victories will win. Instead, it's a short-term marriage where each side will have to give a little in order to achieve their most important goals. To use a football analogy, the best deals are the ones that fall somewhere between the 45-yard lines, indicating that both sides have given in a little, but both have achieved their most important goals. And remember that your broker should do the negotiating for you; you need to protect your relationship with the buyer.

You're not going to win on every point, because the buyer will walk away before you even have the chance. Consult with your advisors to determine what the most critical outcomes are for your situation, and evaluate the issues that will impact those outcomes. Do you need to focus on cash in hand at closing? Is your priority a clean break from the company as soon as possible? Be willing to give on the issues that don't affect your goals. You may even be pleasantly surprised to discover where your interests align with the buyer's. The "Resources for Selling Your Company" section of the book lists materials to help you negotiate the best deal possible.

10. Can I stay on as an employee after I sell?

Sure, in some situations, you can stay with the company as an employee after the sale. The more important question, however, is whether you are sure you want to do that. You've been your own boss for years; do you really want to start working for someone else now, particularly in the company where you're used to making all the decisions? If you haven't enjoyed being an entrepreneur and dislike the stress of running your own company, but still like the industry, perhaps staying as an employee will be an ideal outcome for both parties. But in many cases, it's too difficult an adjustment for former owners to make. Remember, too, that buyers may not want the former owner hanging around and dividing loyalty or creating dissension in the ranks. Finally, examine Chapter 9 to make sure you understand the implications of bank financing; an SBA loan may impact your ability to stay involved in the business.

CHAPTER 8

Top Ten Questions from Buyers

When you find out someone has a baby, there are certain universal questions everyone asks. How old are they? What's their personality like? How is it being a parent? It's the same with buyers of businesses, too: they want to know all about your baby. Buyers can come from a variety of backgrounds, as we cover in Chapter 1. But no matter who (or what) your buyer is, you can count on them asking these questions. And you better have answers!

Typically, these will be among the first questions a buyer asks, before they've made an offer and certainly before due diligence. Don't let these questions scare you—they're not deal killers. That is, they're not deal killers if you have adequate answers. You need to be able to explain the context of your company. And in some cases, you need to jump on the bomb before it explodes on your buyer. Additionally, don't let these questions offend you. The buyer is just trying to find out about the company; they're not trying to criticize your performance as owner.

It's far, far better to address any issues up front, rather than have the buyer uncover them on their own later down the road. If there's an issue with your business—and there will be *multiple* issues — it's ok! Buyers aren't naïve; they understand no company is perfect. And frankly, if your company were perfect, you probably wouldn't be selling it. What buyers want is full disclosure on what the issues are. Buyers are trying to maximize the upside and protect themselves from the downside, which probably isn't so different from how you've been running the company. Addressing issues up front allows you to control the narrative. You can explain the context and thereby frame problems in a more positive light.

Not divulging problems right away is a classic way sellers can kill a sale. Doing so makes you look suspicious and plants a seed of doubt in the buyer's mind. From the buyer's perspective, if you haven't revealed this problem, what else haven't you revealed? Remember that selling a business is not just a quick transaction. It's a short-term marriage where the parties need to get along and work well together. If the buyer is suspicious of you, your relationship will not function well. Ask yourself, "If I were buying this business, what would I want to know about it?" Then volunteer that information and build your credibility with the buyer.

To be clear, you need to be 100 percent honest about the facts of your business. But you also need to be careful not to reveal too much about your opinions and perceptions. You've already decided to sell your company, and you're preparing to walk away. As they begin to distance themselves, many sellers subconsciously develop a negative opinion of the company. You need to remember you're talking to someone who's starting out and has all the energy and enthusiasm you used to have. Don't crush their dreams—and your sale—with unwarranted negativity.

With all that in mind, here are the questions you need to be prepared to answer.

1. How does the business work?

This may seem simplistic to you, but make sure you have patience with the buyer. Remember that most buyers come from different industries and have never worked as owners. And even if they do have some experience in your industry, they're still trying to size up your company and get a feel for the local industry. The buyer is also trying to learn more about you: what you're like as an owner, how well you grasp the business, and how well prepared you'll be to answer the rest of their questions.

Assume the buyer doesn't know much, and draw a pictogram for them. They need to understand the basic business model and what the key factors are that determine success. Cover fundamentals such as finding and converting clients, sourcing materials, delivering products and services, and processing customer payments. All businesses have these processes, but how they work can differ greatly. Most of all, buyers want to know the critical risk points unique to your company. For one clothing manufacturer, their secret to success was the cotton they were able to source from a particular region of the country. Obviously, you don't want to reveal trade secrets that need to be protected with a non-disclosure agreement, but you should be prepared to explain the basics.

2. How long have you been in business?

Sounds simple, right? In a way, it is. But there's a lot more information buyers are trying to suss out when they ask this question. They do want to know how long the company has existed, of course. But they also want to know about the context in which it has existed. Has it survived an economic recession? How did your company, and the industry as a whole, perform? How were you able to navigate it successfully? Think of ways you can put a positive spin on it. Managing through difficult times can actually improve margins as you focus on creating efficiencies and controlling variable costs. Additionally, buyers want to know about the company's stage in its business cycle. Is it still growing? Peaking? Has it experienced any decline?

3. What is your day-to-day role in the company?

Buyers want to know how active the owner is in the day-to-day running of the business. The answer to this question illuminates a lot of related information for the buyer. How essential is the owner to the functioning of the business? How difficult will the transition process be? Are customer and vendor relationships built around personal friendships with the owner, and if so, are they likely to leave when the owner does? If there are critical tasks that only the owner knows how to do, the buyer may plan a more intensive transition process. If the owner plays a critical role in marketing or negotiations, the buyer may have to consider keeping the owner on as an employee for a while after the sale. In the worst case, the buyer may walk away if he believes the company cannot function without the current owner, or if the responsibilities are more than the buyer wants to manage.

Many owners are rightfully proud of the company they've built. Unfortunately, this can lead them to making themselves seem more important than they actually are. One janitorial service company owner claimed he worked sixty hours per week in his company, but at least eight of those hours were actually spent on his twice-weekly trips to the local big box store, browsing the aisles and comparing deals on brooms and toilet paper. Remember that buyers don't want owners to be integral to the company, especially in terms of business functions or marketing. Instead, they want a well-oiled machine where the staff runs the company efficiently and without too much intervention from the owner. Just as we cover in Chapter 4, make sure you've separated yourself from the business so the brand can stand on its own.

4. What is your revenue?

Revenue is a safe place for the buyer to begin a conversation about company financials. As explained in Chapter 1, the vast majority of buyers are individuals. They're trying to make sure your company will earn them a return on their investment and generate enough income to support their families. You should be prepared with three years of clean financial records—at a minimum, the balance sheets and income statements.

By asking about revenue, buyers are looking to establish some standards by which they can compare your company to similar-sized companies in the industry. Eventually, they'll move the discussion into profitability and other financial data. Buyers are also trying to determine whether they'll be able to get financing, either from you or from a bank, for their purchase. After all, buyers generally don't want to pay cash out of pocket. They want to make sure they'll have enough cash left over to run the business and develop it. See Chapter 5 for more information on company financials.

5. What are your employees like?

The buyer may ask about how many employees you have, but what they're really trying to get at is *how* they are. Be prepared to share how long the employees have worked at your company and what staff retention rates are like. Are they smart and hardworking? Are they experienced and able to make good decisions? Do they communicate well? Are they capable of running the business without you, or learning how to do so? Your answers can help the buyer understand what the transition process could be like.

Almost all buyers want to minimize disruption and keep the existing staff. As explained in Chapter 3, many buyers try to generate immediate loyalty by offering new incentives. You can explain your employees' motivation and identify what might resonate with them. You can also help the buyer craft messaging to demonstrate their good intentions and assure employees that things like pay will remain the same.

Buyers also want to know what happens when an employee leaves. You should have a clear HR procedure in place that covers identifying, vetting, hiring, onboarding, and training new employees. Have that procedure documented among your other procedures, such as marketing and sales. It's also helpful if you can share whether any employees are likely to leave upon the change in ownership, perhaps because they've been considering making a change or nearing retirement age. If anyone in your family is working in the business, make sure you have a clear plan for their future.

6. What are your customers like?

There's a lot of hidden depth to this question, too. One of a buyer's biggest concerns is what happens if customers leave. Buyers need to feel out the risk of customers defecting because of an ownership change. And if there is a considerable risk of that, they need to determine the value of that risk so they can adjust their offer. If the new owner of a gym loses twenty members, it probably won't matter much to the bottom line. But if the new owner of a contracting firm loses the customer who accounted for 40 percent of their business, that's a huge chunk.

Buyers want to know in advance what the customer landscape is like. The best way to alleviate a buyer's concerns in this area is to have no customer concentration issues. This means following the advice from Chapter 3 on having a diverse customer base, multiple customer sources, and a comprehensive marketing program. Having this in place will also ease and shorten the transition process and allow the seller to walk away sooner.

7. What is the competitive landscape?

Some buyers, especially first-time business buyers and individuals who worked at large corporations, ask very specific questions about the market that most owners simply don't track. They may want to know your marketing reach, market penetration, or competitor funding. It's okay if you don't have all this data. It's not okay, however, to state that your company is just "better" than the competition. You need to have a real, substantive answer.

Instead, paint a picture of the competitive landscape and how your company fits into it. Who are your major competitors? Are there any secondary competitors, or companies on the rise? What's your differentiator—the thing you do better than anyone that converts customers and keeps them coming back? The buyer *will* do industry research; your job is to help them narrow their search to the most useful comparisons. If you're selling a taco shop in La Jolla, California, the right comparison for them to consider *isn't* all restaurants in San Diego. It's more likely the fast casual Tex-Mex eateries in the greater La Jolla area.

Remember, the buyer will confirm what you tell them, so give them an honest evaluation of your advantages and disadvantages.

They're not expecting your company to be a world beater, but they do want to understand the circumstances of the company they may be buying. Plus, the more good information you share, the more credibility you'll build with the buyer.

8. If you wanted to grow the business, what would you do?

Buyers are looking for a return on their investment. Their purchase decision, therefore, will turn on whether they believe the business has room to grow. No matter how you feel about your business baby—whether you're fed up or still in love—you need to present a company with tons of upside. That's why I said in Chapter 1 that you should avoid selling your company at a peak (and certainly avoid it in a decline!).

Prepare a list of ideas the buyer can consider to grow the company. Smart buyers understand it's difficult to make drastic changes immediately, so you'll want to include a range of opportunities. They'll look for simple steps they can take in the beginning, along with long-term strategies they can pursue down the road.

The initial, straightforward suggestions might include, for example, purchasing another vehicle or more equipment so you can serve more customers at once. The easier the items are to implement, the more excited the buyer will be—who doesn't love instant gratification? Calculate what the costs will be and how it will impact revenue and profitability. Your business broker can help you work out the details. For longer-term projects, you may consider explaining that what the company needs above all is someone to focus on business development. Many buyers see themselves in that role more naturally than the day-to-day operator role.

See Chapter 4 for further explanation on how to identify and frame opportunities for the buyer. Also see Chapter 6 for how you can lay the groundwork for longer-term strategies buyers can develop. Whatever the possibilities, be positive and enthusiastic about them.

9. What hard assets does the company have?

Lots of buyers—especially first-time business buyers—ask this question because they think hard assets will help them secure financing for the purchase. You use your home as collateral for a mortgage, so you need real estate or equipment to serve as collateral for a business loan, right? This is both wrong *and* right. It's true that banks won't collateralize intellectual property, and that having hard assets can help with financing. But lacking hard assets generally isn't an issue in getting a business loan from a bank, because most business loans are guaranteed by the SBA. As a result, the banks care only about the health of the business as revealed in the financial documents.

Don't misunderstand—it's important you're able to list all the assets of your company, both tangible and intangible, that will be included in the sale. This may involve hard assets like real estate, computers, vehicles, and office equipment. And it will certainly involve things like customer lists, content resources, and the like. It may even involve patents and other intellectual property. Buyers want to know exactly what they're getting, and both parties want to be absolutely clear on what is included in the sale. (Identify these items in writing as soon as possible. I've seen deals broken up at the last minute over items as inconsequential as a taxidermy fish hanging on the office wall.) But make sure your buyer understands the company doesn't need tangible assets to qualify for a loan.

10. Why are you selling?

Some buyers are suspicious of why an owner is selling. As discussed, only 20 percent of companies sell, which means it's hard to find a successful company on the market. From these buyers' perspective, if your company is one of the good ones, why would you willingly walk away? They assume there must be something wrong with the business. The best way to answer this is to relate back to the buyer. Most buyers are individuals who come from long careers in the corporate world. After so many years doing that, they've moved on to something new. You're doing the same exact thing!

It's important to phrase your position in a positive way. You could say something like this: "I still love this company and my people, and I still believe in our product, but I don't have the same energy and drive I once did. If someone new with stamina and enthusiasm takes the reins, there are great ways to grow this company! This business and the people deserve more than the limited time and effort I'm willing to contribute at this point."

After hearing this, most buyers will ask what your plans are after the sale. First and foremost, assure them you are not going to be competing with them in any way. Beyond that, it's important to have an answer ready (don't say you haven't decided yet), but it doesn't matter as much what the answer is. Perhaps you will retire, move away, buy a smaller company outside this industry—the world is your oyster, and they're all acceptable answers—but pick one to share with the buyer.

Finally, confirm that you'll be available to teach and train the buyer for whatever amount of time (within reason) is needed, and that you'll be available any time in the future should something unexpected occur that they might want advice on.

In reality, most buyers do not ask for help beyond the transition covered in the sales contract. It's very rare to see a buyer regularly ask the seller questions beyond the agreed-to training period. But if the buyer does come across something a year from now, make them feel comfortable that you will answer your phone or an email to help them if you can. Buyers fear sellers will take the money and run off into the sunset, never to be heard from again. Explain how you want the company, the buyer, the staff, and the customers to continue to do well. It's all part of selling a business.

CHAPTER 9

Top Ten Facts You Need to Know about Bank Financing

Bank financing can be a great benefit for buyer and seller in a business transaction. It means the buyer can come into the deal with less cash (and save the cash they do have for use in the business), while the seller can walk away from closing with more cash. It can also allow for a cleaner separation when the deal closes.

Both the business and the buyer must qualify for the loan. As a seller, you must understand whether your business can qualify for a loan already, or what changes you can make to get it there. Buyers, even those who are walking around with a ton of cash, usually aren't willing to risk it all on the purchase. Happily, banks will finance between 60 and 90 percent of qualified deals, and the buyer funds the majority of the remainder. This allows the seller to walk away with 90 to 100 percent of the purchase price at closing.

If the business can't qualify for a loan and the buyer doesn't have or want to use cash, then the only alternative is seller financing. In those deals, the average seller receives about 50 percent of the purchase price in cash at closing—and may walk away with as little as 30 percent.

Thankfully, the Small Business Administration (SBA) makes it easier than you might think to secure financing to purchase a business. It's a powerful program, and really the reason the United States has a small- to medium-size business transaction market. The SBA provides a guarantee to bank and non-bank lenders across the

US that allows the lender to loan money to small businesses with reduced risk to the lender. The SBA requires competitive rates and fees of these lenders and helps keep requirements reasonable. It's a win-win for everyone. Ultimately, a large percentage of deals are bank-financed, and you should aim to be one of them.

1. Almost No Business Financing Is Done Conventionally

The SBA's motto is "to ignite change and spark action so small businesses can confidently start, grow, expand, or recover." And they live up to it: Just about every business deal is funded through SBA programs. It's a common myth that the SBA loans money. In fact, banks loan the money. The SBA guarantees the loan, so the bank knows it will get paid back even if the buyer defaults. The SBA guarantees a large portion of a deal, and banks gladly seize the opportunity to make money with far less risk.

If your buyer says they plan to use conventional financing, your eyebrows should raise. It may mean they're inexperienced and don't know much about the process. What bank would finance with a conventional loan, where they carry all of the risk, when they could finance with an SBA loan, where they carry almost none of the risk? Chances are the buyer hasn't looked into it. The only time it ever really happens is when the buyer has a cash deposit at the bank equal to the amount of the conventional loan.

2. Most Eligibility Requirements Are from the Bank, Not the SBA

The SBA places fairly minimal requirements on loans. A business needs to be a US-based, for-profit company that qualifies as a small business (size requirements vary by industry). Some industries aren't eligible, like lending and life insurance. It also can't be in certain "sin industries" like gambling. A person needs to be free of government debt defaults, bankruptcy in the last ten years, and certain types of criminal history. Based on SBA guidelines alone, most companies and people qualify. Banks, however, are allowed to implement their own additional guidelines, and it's these requirements that tend to cause the most disqualifications. Just because one bank says you're not qualified for their SBA loans doesn't mean your business won't qualify for another bank's SBA loans. Shop around!

3. Both Business and Buyer Must Qualify

When deciding whether to fund a business transaction, the bank evaluates both the company and the buyer. As mentioned above, besides meeting the basic SBA requirements, the bank can impose its own unique requirements on each party as well. Sellers can get their businesses pre-qualified, which can help draw in buyers (who hopefully also qualify!).

There are some basic limits that almost all banks impose. Generally, banks won't touch a company unless it:

- Has two years of clean books and records (see Chapter 5 for more on financials)
- Is profitable—and isn't experiencing declining profitability
- Has been in business for at least two years

Banks also must manage some practical realities. There's a cost to doing these deals, so it can be more difficult to fund a small deal than a large one. If the loan is for under $250,000, there's often just not enough profit in it for the bank to justify the work involved.

4. Banks Do Not Care That This Business Is Your Baby

Let me repeat: banks do not care that this business is your baby. They don't care how much you love it and how much potential it has. Remember, it's not personal. Consider the situation from the perspective of the bank: their number-one concern is reducing the risk of default. They're interested in dollars and cents, so that's what they'll examine to make their funding decision. Banks use the SBA guarantee, the buyer's down payment, and additional collateral (such as seller financing and hard assets) to make sure they'll get repaid.

Most banks are cash flow lenders, meaning they'll look at the company's EBITDA (earnings before interest, taxes, depreciation, and amortization) to see how much money the business is making. Then they'll use a debt ratio to determine how much debt the company can afford. Some people mistakenly believe banks will only lend on hard assets like real estate, but that's not true. When considering business loans, banks look at profitability. Other assets like real estate are beneficial, but not necessary.

5. Use Accrual Accounting

I commented on the choice between accrual and cash accounting in Chapters 2 and 5, but it deserves another mention. Accrual accounting records transactions (expenses and revenue) when they occur, but not necessarily when they are paid. By contrast, cash accounting records transactions when they are paid, but not necessarily when they occur.

Here is a simple scenario to illustrate the difference: a customer buys a product from you on October 1, on a thirty-day payment term. The customer then pays you on November 1. Accrual accounting would record the sale on October 1 (when the transaction occurred), whereas cash accounting would record the sale on November 1 (when the transaction was paid for).

It may seem like a subtle difference, but it matters a great deal. Banks strongly prefer accrual accounting. They believe it paints a more accurate picture of the company's cycles and expenses. Your accountant may encourage you to stick with cash accounting for tax purposes, but banks (and sellers) will expect to see accrual accounting—and it very well could influence their decision on your company.

6. Bank Financing Extends Deal Closing

Keep the timeline clear in your mind: you need at least (at least!) six months, and preferably two years, to prepare your company before you put it on the market. Then it'll take months to find a buyer.

Then you enter negotiations and agree to terms. Finally, you can pick a closing date. When the conditions are right (buyer and seller are motivated, there are no complicating factors, there's no bank financing), business transaction deals can close quickly, which means between thirty and sixty days from agreeing to terms until close. Those conditions, however, are rarely met.

Whatever closing date you'd like, you'll need to add thirty to ninety additional days if you're using bank financing. The national average of eight and a half months to find a buyer and close a deal assumes bank financing. But if you need to sell the business quickly (say, thirty to sixty days), using bank financing may not be possible.

Also realize there's a heavy bank bureaucracy involved in getting these deals approved and funded. You may be able to save time by choosing the right bank. It's important to select a bank with experience doing SBA acquisition loans, as they'll have the knowledge and established processes to get the job done as quickly as possible. It's also to your advantage to work with a bank that's been certified as a preferred lender with the SBA. This allows the bank to self-approve SBA loans, rather than submitting the paperwork to the SBA and waiting on their approval—which, as you might imagine, can take forever.

7. Be Careful with Deal Structure

Bank financing can impact how a transaction deal is structured. Banks are all about numbers, so they like when deals have a definitive purchase price. They disfavor earnouts because it means the value of the business will vary based on future performance, which makes it harder to accurately value the business now. As a result, very few banks will finance a deal with an earnout component.

Now, this doesn't mean the buyer and seller can't establish an earnout-like structure. Banks finance between 60 and 90 percent of the deal, so 10 to 40 percent of the purchase price still needs to be funded by the buyer and/or seller. That portion of the deal can be financed via seller financing using various deal terms and structures, some of which even achieve the same outcome as an earnout. In fact, banks often like having seller financing to accompany the loan.

8. Bank Financing Doesn't Eliminate Seller Financing

More and more, banks will actually ask the seller to hold part of the financing of the deal, often 20 to 30 percent. The bank wants to eliminate risk, so they want 100 percent collateral coverage. In addition to reducing risk on that portion of the money, seller financing also gives the bank security that the prior owner will help with the transition process. It's not that the bank wants the prior owner to stay involved in the business (read the next point for more on that). Rather, the bank wants to know the prior owner will be available to the buyer when the buyer needs information, advice, or help. If the seller has skin in the game, they're more likely to support the buyer.

9. Sellers Cannot Stay Involved for More Than One Year

When a bank finances a deal, it requires both the company and the buyer to be qualified. The new owner is the one who made the deal with the bank and who owes the money, so the bank wants the new owner to be the one in full control. Therefore, banks (and the SBA) stipulate that sellers cannot retain equity or be involved as an employee or consultant as of one year after the closing. If the seller wants to stay on as an employee or remain otherwise involved in the company, bank financing probably isn't an option.

10. Your Company Should Look Better than Ever at Closing

Whatever stage of the sale process a company is in, owners need to be crystal clear on their priorities. Their single most important job is *not* working on the sale—it is running the company well.

The day your company gets approved for a loan will give you all the warm and fuzzies. The cold, numbers-obsessed bank thinks your baby is beautiful! That's great, but the loan process does not stop with approval. The bank will continue to ask for updated financials. They may even request running comparisons between this year and last year throughout the closing process. Up until the day of closing, the bank can still ask you for the latest thirty- or ninety-day financial report. In some industries, they may require information about backlogs and future contracted revenue. The bank expects to see stability (preferably growth!) in revenue and profit. If they're not satisfied with the company's performance, they will pull out of the loan—and possibly kill the deal.

CHAPTER 10

Top Ten Mistakes When Selling a Business

We've made it a long way together through this book. You now have a baseline knowledge on how businesses are valued and sold, how to increase the likelihood of selling, and how to maximize purchase price. But we're not out of the woods yet. No matter how much knowledge a seller has, there are key tripping points that can turn a deal south fast. Although I can't include every mistake sellers have made, these are the top ten most common mistakes we see with small to medium business sales.

1. Unrealistic Expectations

Now that you've read this book, you understand what to expect when selling your company. You've absorbed the information about prepping your finances, understanding your ideal buyer, and evaluating purchase options. You've learned how to avoid deal killers and how to manage your employees and customers.

But you still probably have some hesitation. Your company—it really is *great*. You've built it meticulously, your team is the best in the region, your product is superior, customers are locked in—any outsider could see the value. Other businesses with less careful owners or inferior staff may have trouble selling, but you really will be fine. Right?

Wrong. The biggest mistake owners make is believing their company is different. Sorry to be the bearer of bad news, but you and your company are not special. You may hear stories in the media about unicorns that sell for thirty times their revenue. This will not happen to you. To say there's a one in a million chance would actually be an improvement over the reality. In fact, the chances of your business selling *at all* is only 20 percent. And the chances of it attracting unicorn prices are practically incalculable, but I'll approximate it at about one in a bajillion. It's just not going to happen.

Your company will—or won't—sell based on the elements covered in this book. If you go into this process with unrealistic expectations, you won't just be disappointed emotionally; you'll actually decrease your chances of selling. You'll be more likely to ask for an unrealistic price or to refuse good offers. You'll lengthen the sales process, and the longer a company sits on the market, the more opportunity there is for something to go wrong. Having realistic expectations isn't just necessary for managing your emotions; it's necessary to make a sale happen.

Finally, realize that selling your business is very different from selling a home. About 98 percent of those who say they want to buy a house will eventually buy one. In the business market, only about 6 percent of those who say they want to buy a company actually do it. Potential homebuyers regularly lowball on price and hope for a negotiation. Business sales transactions include negotiations on lots of deal elements, and price is just one of them. In fact, buyers are far more likely either to offer a reasonable price or to make no offer at all. Additionally, price fluctuates far more dramatically in business sales than in home sales. As long as your house doesn't burn down overnight, what it's worth today is basically what it'll be worth tomorrow. In business valuation, however, one public faux pas by the owner can render a company worthless overnight. Ultimately, real estate is far more liquid than a business, and the markets are very different, so don't expect a similar process.

2. Trying to Go It Alone

It's incredibly difficult to run a business. You know, because you've been doing it for years. Leading a company—even a well-performing one—is time-consuming and stressful. Now imagine having another full-time job on top of it. Sound exhausting? That's what you're asking for if you think you can manage the sales process on your own.

At a bare minimum, your company needs to run at least as well on the day the deal closes as it does today. And even that might not be enough. Really, you should be able to demonstrate growth, increased efficiency, and improved profitability throughout the sales process. After all, that's how you attract more buyers and higher sales prices. In fact, during the year (or more) you're on the market and closing the deal, you need to work harder on your business than you ever have before.

Most business owners are already overworked. Asking them to improve the company, get all the financials in order, market the company, vet potential buyers, draft a contract, and negotiate a deal is far, far too much for one person. Nothing good can come of it. You're likely either to falter in running the company or make a big mistake in the sales process. Both of these lead to the same outcomes: the reduced value of your business, and a lower likelihood of completing a sale.

Additionally, many parts of the sales process require specialized, technical knowledge that the vast majority of business owners lack. Do you know how to market a company confidentially? Structure a bank loan to maximize the cash in your pocket on the day of closing? Write a contract that protects you from future lawsuits? Organize the deal and your finances so you don't have to pay huge amounts in unnecessary taxes? Even if these specialists cost you some money up front, it's nothing compared to the money you could lose if you don't engage them. Revisit Chapter 2 for information on how to surround yourself with the right advisory team.

3. Focusing on the Offer That Landed in Your Inbox

I'm about to burst some bubbles. The email that landed in your inbox this morning, the one from the private equity firm fawning about how great your business is and how much they would love to buy your company? It was a mass email sent to thousands of companies like yours across the country. It's a professional phishing expedition to try to get you to limit your buyer pool to one party: their firm. Worse, it could be an attempt to learn information about your company they'll then use to improve the deal with the company they're *really* interested in buying. For the offers that are real, they may not be lowballs, but they likely are not the most advantageous deal structure for sellers.

The lesson here is not to limit your buyer pool. Sellers who limit their buyer pool cap the value they'll receive for their business. There are a number of ways this can happen. Many sellers are so relieved to get an offer at all that they jump at the first one they get. Some will receive an unsolicited offer like the one described above from a private equity (PE) firm or strategic buyer and think they've hit the jackpot. Others have always assumed they'll sell to an employee or their child. All of these scenarios should be approached with caution.

Certainly it's a great day when you put your company on the market and you receive an offer. But don't sign on the dotted line without carefully evaluating your options. Of course, if you've done the prep work, vetted the buyer, and find the terms acceptable (or even terrific!), don't reject it because you're suddenly convinced you have a unicorn on your hands—you don't. In fact, you may never receive as good an offer ever again. Remember, the only way you'll know if an offer is once-in-a-lifetime is if you've already done the exit prep work with your advisors.

Some owners plan to sell their company to a key employee or pass it on to the next generation of their family. Unfortunately, many owners make these plans in their heads without ever actually discussing it with the employee or family member at issue. Selling to these types of buyers can be wonderful for the legacy of your company. But have you asked them whether they can afford the company—or if they even want to own it? As entrepreneurs, we know this job isn't as glamorous as it seems. Not everyone is cut out to own their own business, and if they are, they're less likely to be working for you in the first place. These next generation and internal buyers often require deals that limit the cash the seller receives on closing day because they have less cash or ability to qualify for a loan than an outside party would. And if this buyer doesn't want or can't afford the company, many owners are devastated and lose interest in their company, which takes a major toll on the value of the business, and subsequently their retirement. You must work with your broker and advisors in advance to prepare exit strategies!

4. Fixating on Valuation Instead of Cash

There's a trend in business sales where sellers love to announce the valuation the buyer gave the company at sale. It's understandable. It sounds awesome to say the buyers thought your company—your baby!—was worth $50 million!

These sellers lose sight of the fact that the *valuation* assigned to the company is very different from the *value* the seller receives at closing. A seller can't spend a valuation; they can only spend the cash they receive in light of that valuation. And even if your company receives a valuation of $50 million, there's almost no chance you're walking away from the closing table with $50 million in your pocket.

Buyers may position their offer to take advantage of the seller's ego—and make no mistake, it's pure ego on the part of the sellers. These buyers structure a deal where the valuation is high, but the seller only gets a small percentage of that valuation at closing. The rest of the valuation *can* be earned—but isn't guaranteed—through structures like earnouts. And these earnouts are often unfavorable for the seller because they leave key business decisions in the hands of the buyer, which reduces the seller's ability to reach the earnout threshold.

Of course, entrepreneurs tend to be naturally optimistic. It would be difficult to start a business otherwise! But they need to be realistic when selling their companies, and protect themselves from the downside. One company sold for a valuation of $20 million dollars, but the sellers only got 10 percent in cash at closing. To earn the rest, the seller had to stay with the company for three years at a minimal salary. After he paid off the debt he'd been carrying on the business and paid taxes, he received only about $1 million cash at closing. After the three-year period, he hit some of the earnout thresholds, but not all, and only received $4 million additional, for a total value of $5 million. He would have been far better off to go with the buyer who assigned a $7 million valuation to the company, but agreed to pay 90 percent in cash at closing and allowed him to move on from the company.

5. Not Having an Attorney

People love to hate attorneys. They can be expensive, egotistical . . . you name it. But selling your company is probably the single largest transaction of your entire life. Are you sure you want to jump off that cliff without an attorney?

In the modern world, handshake deals no longer really exist. There are all kinds of bad actors in business, and "reputable" people renege on deals or screw over their partners all the time. You may dislike them, but a good attorney is worth their weight in gold. Even if they don't get you a better price at the negotiating table, they still protect you from the downside, which can be a very scary place.

Many sellers don't know they need an attorney until it's already far too late. Selling a business is not just a simple exchange of assets. It's a complex legal transaction that requires regular work in the field to know how to structure properly. There are ownership structure choices, licensing requirements, copyright protections, and a million more issues that can arise. Even if you've handled all the legal matters for your company since you founded it—heck, even if you're an actual attorney—you're still not necessarily qualified to act as an attorney in a business sale.

The following situation demonstrates danger for the buyer instead of the seller, but the principle of needing an attorney holds true. A buyer bought an e-commerce company for $60,000. He did all the paperwork himself, believing that the deal was too small to involve a lawyer. A few years later, he was sued by a Fortune 500 company, which used attorneys from a prestigious, high-powered law firm. After the seller sold the business to the buyer, he took the computer code he used to build the company and sold it to a different buyer. Eventually, that code ended up in the hands of the Fortune 500 company, which acted litigiously when they discovered the original buyer was also using the code. In an effort to save a few bucks, the buyer found himself in a heap of legal trouble.

Keep in mind that a broker is *not* an adequate substitute for an attorney. A broker could probably structure a deal better than you could, but that's not saying much. If you can have only one outside advisor in the whole process, it must be a business transaction attorney.

6. Not Keeping It Confidential

Selling a business is a long, sometimes painful process. It's difficult and emotional. After all, you're selling your baby. It would be nice to talk to one of your employees, vendors, or customers about it; they've been in the trenches with you and are the ones most likely to understand. But part of your job as a leader is protecting your baby and those people who have helped raise it. You need to shield them from the roller coaster you endure every day, just like you would with cash flow issues or other significant challenges you face daily as a business owner.

Entrepreneurs are designed differently from most other people. You're made for the wild ride, whereas others need the comfort of working for someone else. You've learned that only about 20 percent of businesses sell, and that half of those under contract still fall through. To you, that may be exhilarating. To the average person, it is terrifying. Employees want to know their company will be there the next day and that their job is secure. Customers want to know they'll be able to rely on you. Recall the story from Chapter 2 in which a gym owner lost 50 percent of his staff overnight when they found out about a potential sale; your employees and customers will leave if word gets out the company is on the market. The surprise announcement of a completed sale can have a happy ending for everyone, but the details that lead up to the deal cannot be exposed. Most buyers don't want to change anything, but employees and customers will always assume the worst.

Additionally, many owners think everyone will be shocked when they find out the business has been sold. In reality, most people aren't. If you're around retirement age or approaching burnout, most people understand and take it in stride—when they find out after the transaction is closed. They don't feel betrayed or abandoned. But that's because they're presented with complete information after the deal is done and a plan is in place. They wouldn't be calm at all if they knew about it leading up to the sale. Read on . . .

7. Lack of Support Systems

Just because entrepreneurs are made for the gauntlet of running their own business doesn't mean it's easy. As discussed above, it's critical not to reveal the sale to employees, clients, vendors, or anyone else involved. Unfortunately, this often leaves the owner to process a great deal all on their own.

While they may achieve superhuman feats of business, entrepreneurs need support just like regular humans. It can be helpful to discuss the sales process with your business partner or a spouse, but even that can be an incomplete solution, as there's so much money and emotion on the line and the partner or spouse is still a stakeholder in the transaction. In my experience, owners with external support systems fare far better through the sales process than those without.

There's absolutely a connection between having good support and getting a better deal. You need a mentor, entrepreneurial support group, executive coach, or even a therapist to go through this process with you. Inevitably, the deal will be on the verge of death at least three times during the sales process. When these times come, you cannot act on emotion. You need to keep a cool head and maintain a relationship with the buyer. Instead, let the brokers and attorneys do their jobs and resurrect the deal. Owners with support can weather those storms; those without can kill the deal beyond salvation.

Your behavior during the difficult times can determine the outcome of the deal. One owner finally found a buyer after struggling for more than a year to identify one. She was tightly wound after working so hard on both the company and the sales process, and she had no one but her husband to turn to for emotional support. The buyer was excited about the company and made a good offer, with one caveat: the buyer wanted to keep the company's existing phone number, which doubled as the owner's cell number. Under normal circumstances, this would be the least onerous condition of all time. For this owner, however, it was the last straw. This was the item that finally broke her after struggling for so long. She got into an actual yelling match with the buyer over a *phone number*. Of course the deal fell apart. When the owner came to her senses a few days later and tried to agree to the offer, the buyer wasn't willing to work with her anymore.

You may read this story and say, "Oh, that's so extreme. It would never happen to me." Don't be so sure. When you endure punch after punch, over and over, for so long, you don't know how you're going to react when you're pushed just a little too far. Remember from the Introduction the story of my near mental breakdown over blow-drying my hair? You never know what will set you off! If you're going to survive the sale process, you need an established support system to keep you sane and even-keeled. And if you remember nothing else from this section, remember the twenty-four-hour rule. If there comes a time when you are stressed, tired, or pissed off about the deal and feel a rage blackout coming on, walk away for twenty-four hours. Cool down, get some rest, and regain some perspective. Only then should you respond.

8. Not Doing the Pre-Sale Prep Work

Many owners don't think about selling until the day they wake up and decide they're done. That's fine, but you should understand reality: you will not receive full value for your company if you do not prepare for sale well before you start thinking about moving on. There are two stages of preparation: building exit options and establishing an exit strategy.

While you're happily running the company and nowhere near thinking about selling, you need to start establishing some exit options for yourself. This doesn't mean deciding that you'll sell in ten years, retire at age sixty-five, pass the company on to your child, or anything else definitive. It just means you're protecting yourself from the possible downsides of a quick exit.

Think about it like diversifying your financial portfolio. You don't know what's going to happen in your life or in the market. Therefore, you put money in a variety of investment vehicles and make sure you have good insurance. Similarly, you need to set up your company in a way that would allow you to sell it at any time if you needed to, however remote the possibility. Consider how you might get value by selling assets like real estate, customer lists, or intellectual property. Set up your personal finances such that you won't have to take a huge tax hit if you sell (some of these strategies require five years of prep time—talk to your financial advisor!). Determine whether your child or a key employee wants to carry on the business, and if so, start training them. Maintain clean business books so you don't have to slog through years of disorganized financial data when you need to sell. Work with an exit strategist or consultant to understand all your options.

The second phase of preparation is establishing your exit strategy. Do this when you're ready to make a decision about exactly when and how you'd like to exit the company. You now have a defined goal, so you need a specific strategy to get there. I've said it over and over and I'll say it again: You need to engage in a systematic, thorough pre-sale preparatory process. Enroll in Exit Factor's Prep to Sell course, which is designed based on industry best practices, our collective decades of experience, and the latest market data. Even if you don't take a course, at least have a broker give you a valuation of the business; it will help you define realistic expectations and give you a starting point for improvement.

9. Not Considering Your Landlord

There's a joke in the business brokerage community. It's the Ls that kill deals: Lawyers, Lenders, and Landlords. You may not get it, but it *slays* at broker meetings.

When you go into business, most owners are energized and enthusiastic. And one of the first, most exciting things you do is find a location for your company and sign a lease. It's a tangible, public sign that your business is really happening, and it can be exhilarating! Unfortunately, the fun ends there. In my years as an entrepreneur and exit strategist, some of the biggest mistakes I've seen business owners make are in their leases. Almost without exception, leases are structured to the significant advantage of the landlord, at the expense of the tenant.

Frankly, most commercial real estate agents aren't on your side, either. They may be working as your representative, but there are other issues at play. First, the landlord pays the agent's commission, not you. It may be unconscious on their part, but the agent will naturally feel some loyalty to the one who signs their paychecks. Second, most commercial real estate agents are not lawyers. They'll be able to explain the basic terms and rates, but they may not fully understand all the legal implications of the lease you're signing.

Among the most important elements in the lease is the assignment clause, which dictates when and how (and if!) a tenant can transfer their lease to another party. Obviously, this can be a critical element in the sale of a company. Most assignment clauses are generic, short, and vague; they lull you to sleep with their seeming innocence. But therein lies the problem! The less definitive the assignment process, the more power your landlord has over it.

I've seen wild scenarios play out when landlords exercise their assignment authority. They've forced closings to extend by as much as six months. They've required sellers to stay on the lease as personal guarantors of the new tenants' rent. In one case, a landlord demanded a commission on the sale of the company! All of these actions were both legal and within the terms of the lease agreement—and therefore all of them could have been avoided.

So what is an owner to do? In an ideal world, you have an attorney examine your lease before you ever sign it so you're protected from any possible assignment shenanigans. If you're already locked into a lease, there are still actions you can take to make the landlord more likely to work with you. First, establish a good relationship with your landlord going into the sale. Ensure you're in compliance with all lease terms and that you're up to date on all your payments. Second, have an attorney examine your lease so you understand what you may be faced with during the sales process. Business brokers and business transactions attorneys probably have worked with landlords in your area, and may be able to tell you what you can expect. Third, don't reveal to your landlord that you're selling the company until the appropriate time. Your broker and attorney will help you identify what that time is, but it certainly won't be before you find a buyer. Most landlords are impatient, and if they think you're having trouble selling the company, they may be tempted to find a new tenant and kick you out rather than have you close up shop and leave them with an empty unit. Remember, the lease agreement is probably heavily weighted in favor of the landlord, so you likely have little recourse if the landlord does this to you.

Finally, remember that if you own your building, then you have a landlord too—you! Preparing for sale means you need to prepare your company *and* decide what to do with the space. Will you lease it back to the buyer or sell it to them? Either way, be realistic about what the business can afford in rent or mortgage. No one knows that better than you!

10. Skipping the Post-Sale Celebration!

If it hasn't become crystal clear yet, selling a business is hard. Really hard. It's exhausting and emotional and stressful. Many entrepreneurs have spent so much time wrapped up in their companies that they lack much of an identity outside of work. Don't let this happen to you. While you're going through this process, it's important to have the sense that you're running *towards* something new, rather than running *away* from something else.

Once I decided to sell my first company, I couldn't wait to get rid of it. Yet the day after closing, I was stunned by the feeling of loss. What was I going to do all day? Who was I, even? I hadn't set up anything to engage me once the sale was done, and it was a real mistake. Way too many sellers get so focused on the process and the day-to-day that they forget to look up and realize that one day soon, there will be no more work to focus on.

You've accomplished something truly remarkable, something that only the elite 20 percent of all owners are able to do—sell their business! It's important to mark the occasion. Against all odds, you grew, successfully ran, and ultimately sold a small business. You are the embodiment of the American dream. So go sail around the world or take the fabulous Caribbean vacation you've always dreamed of. (By the way, even if you're staying on in the business as an employee or helping with the transition process, you can still take a vacation. Just make sure the buyer knows before the deal closes!)

I helped an older couple sell their company for several million dollars. They were set up for a luxurious retirement. When I asked them how they were going to reward themselves for all their hard work, they immediately and enthusiastically answered, "We're going to Red Lobster!" However you like to celebrate, go wild—but maybe push your imagination a little further than the local restaurant chain down the street!

Resources for Selling Your Company

No owner should go through the business sales process alone. There's simply too much to do and too much specialized knowledge required. Nonetheless, the more an owner understands about the process, the better they'll be able to make decisions and prioritize tasks.

You'll notice there are no legal resources included on this list. That's because *you need to get a business transactions lawyer*. Hold your nose if you must, but hire one ASAP.

ADVISORS AND BROKERS

It's incredibly difficult to sell a company without a broker. If you don't want to go to a broker right away, consider starting the sales exploration process with an experienced small business advisor.

- Transworld Business Advisors is the largest business brokerage in the United States. It's helped tens of thousands of entrepreneurs achieve their dreams of buying or selling a company. Find your local office at tworld.com.
- The International Business Brokers Association (IBBA) is the premier association for qualified business brokers. Visit ibba.org to search by area and qualification to find the best fit for you.
- The Small Business Administration has a database of low cost and free advisors. Access it at sba.gov/local-assistance.
- Our list of advisors on exitfactor.com.

FINANCIALS

Many business owners simply do not understand the financials in their company. If you want to get the most value for your business, you need to dig into these numbers and learn from them.

- *Simple Numbers, Straight Talk, Big Profits!: 4 Keys to Unlock Your Business*, by Greg Crabtree. This is the seminal text on the subject, and I highly recommend it.
- *The Ultimate Blueprint for an Insanely Successful Business,* by Keith Cunningham
- *Financial Intelligence: A Manager's Guide to Knowing What the Numbers Really Mean,* by Karen Berman and Joe Wright

GROWING YOUR BUSINESS

These books are the three most commonly used guides to building a successful company. Their processes will help you create an efficient, profitable company for the long term, and will help you attract lots of buyers who want to pay top dollar for what you've built.

- *Scaling Up: How a Few Companies Make It . . . and Why the Rest Don't (Rockefeller Habits 2.0)*, by Verne Harnish
- *Traction: Get a Grip on Your Business*, by Gino Wickman
- *The E-Myth Revisited: Why Most Small Businesses Don't Work and What to Do About It*, by Michael E. Gerber

MARKET RESEARCH

Before you sell, you need to get a sense of the market. What else is for sale? What's the market like in my industry? Are there any competitors for sale? How do I match up to what's out there?

- BizBuySell is a great place to browse businesses for sale around the country. Access their listings and other resources at bizbuysell.com/insight-report/.

- Bizminer allows you to compare your company's performance and expenses against other similarly sized companies in your industry. Access their data at bizminer.com.
- Your local advisor should also have access to a list of regional companies on the market.

NEGOTIATION AND GETTING DEALS DONE

Remember that you don't need to win all the points, just the important ones.

- *Closing the Deal*, by Andrew Cagnetta
- *Never Split the Difference,* by Chris Voss

PEOPLE

Perhaps the greatest asset in your company is the people. You need to make sure you've got the right employees on your team.

- *Who*, by Geoff Smart and Randy Street, can help business owners solve the chronic problem of unsuccessful hiring.
- *The Business Playbook: How to Document and Delegate What You Do So Your Company Can Grow Beyond You*, by Chris Ronzio
- *Taking Point: A Navy SEAL's 10 Fail Safe Principles for Leading Through Change,* by Brent Gleeson
- It's also mentioned above, but Verne Harnish's *Scaling Up* is an excellent guide to building a functional team.

SALES PREPARATION PROCESS

If you're going to sell your business, you need to engage in a comprehensive preparatory course. There are plenty available online.

- Our Prep to Sell course delivered through Exit Factor. Check it out at exitfactor.com.

- *The Deal Board* podcast, where Transworld CEO Andrew Cagnetta and I gather weekly to share tips on buying and selling businesses and discuss industry trends. It's available anywhere you listen to podcasts.

VALUATION

Most business owners are badly disappointed when they discover what their company is actually worth. You need to establish realistic expectations before you undertake the sales process.

- Transworld Business Advisors has a Business Valuation Calculator that helps business owners determine what their company might sell for on the open market. Find it at tworld.com/sell-a-business/calculator.
- BizBuySell publishes a quarterly Insight Report that tracks the health of the US small business market. It offers a ton of useful information broken down by industry and region, and is available at bizbuysell.com/insight-report.

SUPPORT

Every entrepreneur needs support, whether on business struggles or emotional issues.

There are a number of highly respected peer groups and coaching networks worth exploring:

- Entrepreneurs' Organization (EO): hub.eonetwork.org
- YPO: ypo.org
- Scaling Up Coaches: coaches.scalingup.com
- Vistage Executive Coaching: vistage.com

You also need to have regular, healthy outlets to help manage stress. Do these activities instead of yelling at the buyer, your advisors, or even your spouse. If you don't know where to start, these may spark some ideas:

- Pretend you're punching the object of your ire in the face at Title Boxing Club: titleboxingclub.com/locations
- Knock the fuzz off a tennis ball at a USTA facility: usta.com/en/home/play/facility-listing.html
- Whack a golf ball at Topgolf: topgolf.com/us/locations/
- Find your local gun range, rage room, or batting cage
- Practice the 24-hour rule: never respond to triggering events for 24 hours

TREAT YO' SELF

Selling your company is a big deal, and worth celebrating. It's also an important way to mark the end of one adventure and the beginning of a new one.

- Go on a safari with National Geographic Expeditions: nationalgeographic.com/expeditions
- Sail around the world with the Ritz Carlton Yacht Collection: ritzcarltonyachtcollection.com
- Relax in style with Inspirato Luxury Properties: inspirato.com

Glossary of Useful Terms

Here is a list of important business terms, many of which we use in the book. You can find more detailed descriptions and a ton more useful terms at exitfactor.com/glossary.

Adjusted Earnings: The money a business makes after adjustments for one-time or extraordinary expenses, such as excess owner compensation, discretionary expenses, and any other expenses that are not essential for the successful ongoing operation of the business. The term is used with SDE or EBITDA, as in Adjusted SDE or Adjusted EBITDA.

Amortization: The "A" in EBITDA. It's the money owed for something (typically intangible, like a loan) that is paid off by making regular payments over a long period of time.

Asking Price: The price at which a business is offered for sale by an owner.

Asset Sale: A form of business acquisition where a buyer and seller agree to transfer some of the assets from the seller's entity to the buyer's entity. In an asset sale, the actual corporate entity is not transferred.

Balance Sheet: One of the two main types of financial documents. The balance sheet shows the company's assets, liabilities, and shareholder equity at a specific moment in time.

Business Broker: A professional business advisor who acts as an intermediary by facilitating the sale of a small- to medium-sized business. Brokers may also be referred to as business intermediaries or transactional advisors.

Capital Structure: The mix of cash, invested equity, and debt that is used to finance the operations of a business.

Cash Flow: A measure of a company's financial performance. It can be calculated multiple ways, but in the context of business transactions, it most often refers to the amount of monetary benefit an entrepreneur receives from owning a business. The term can be used interchangeably with Seller's Discretionary Earnings (SDE) or Discretionary Earnings (DE), which is one of the earnings numbers that can be used to calculate a business valuation.

Customer Base: Who your customers are, how many you have, what industries they're in, and how you find them. The wider and deeper your customer base, the better.

Deal Structure: The combination of types of payment by which the purchase of a business is accomplished. It can include cash, loans, stock, consulting agreements, earnout provisions, and non-compete agreements.

Due Diligence (DD): The process, or the period during which the process is conducted, of sharing information from the seller to the buyer of a business for the purpose of evaluation and verification of statements made by the seller and their advisors.

Earnout: The portion of the purchase price that is contingent on a future event. That future event could be the performance of the business at predefined specific levels of a financial metric such as sales or profit.

EBITDA: Earnings before interest, taxes, depreciation, and amortization. A financial measure used to determine overall business performance for the purpose of valuation. This metric can be used instead of Seller's Discretionary Earnings (SDE) for larger businesses or those with a management team in place.

Fair Market Value: The value for which a company would sell on the open market when a willing seller and a willing buyer come to terms when neither is under duress.

Financial Documents: The two main financial documents are the balance sheet and income statement. Other important financial documents may include tax returns and bank statements.

Financial Recasting: The process of adjusting expenses or revenue to reflect only those items which are essential and necessary in a business. Used in valuation of small businesses when there are unnecessary, one-time, or personal expenses included in the business' financial documents. Also referred to as adjustments or add-backs.

Goodwill: The amount by which the price paid for a company exceeds the company's adjusted book value of the underlying tangible assets and liabilities. Goodwill is a result of name, reputation, customer loyalty, location, products, and net income.

Income Statement: One of the two main types of financial documents. It reports the company's financial performance over a certain period of time and explains how revenue turns into earnings. It reveals how much overhead the company has and how much it costs to produce the goods you sell. Also called a profit and loss statement, or P&L.

Letter of Intent (LOI): A written statement, signed before the due diligence period, of the intention to enter into a formal sales agreement after due diligence. It lays out the basic terms of the deal.

Multiple: In the context of buying and selling businesses, a multiple is applied to a company's earnings number (either SDE or EBITDA) to determine the valuation.

Non-Disclosure Agreement (NDA): A legal contract between two parties (the seller and the buyer) that outlines confidential information the parties wish to share with one another but not with any third parties.

Private Equity Firm: A collection of investors that may look to buy a business, combine it with other companies, grow them together, and then sell. Typically, they are interested in companies with over $1 million in annual EBITDA.

Projection: Prospective financial statements that present a business's expected revenues, expenses, and earnings in the future.

Purchase Price: The amount of money a buyer pays for a business. It generally consists of a combination of cash, buyer financing through a bank, and seller financing, and may include an earnout or adjustable note.

Return on Investment (ROI): A profitability measure that evaluates company performance by dividing net profit by net worth. Buyers look to buy companies that will generate a reasonable ROI.

SBA Loan: A loan, given by a bank, guaranteed by the SBA (Small Business Administration).

Seller's Discretionary Earnings (SDE): Seller's discretionary earnings is the total benefit an owner receives from a small business. It is calculated by adding interest, depreciation and amortization, owner's compensation, owner's benefits, and non-recurring expenses to the net income before taxes (operating income) of the company. Can be used interchangeably with Cash Flow.

Seller Financing: A loan provided by the seller to the buyer that will be paid back over a specific time period at a specified interest rate.

Stock Sale: A form of acquisition whereby all or a portion of the stock in a corporation is sold to the purchaser.

Strategic Buyers: Businesses that look to grow by buying other, slightly smaller companies in the same or a related industry.

Transaction Value: Total consideration (or value) paid for a business when transferring ownership from a buyer to a seller.

Valuation: What a company is worth. It is based on the financials of the company and can be calculated in a variety of ways, including discounted cash flow method, asset method, and, most popular, market method.

Working Capital: The excess of current assets over current liabilities.